HACKING
FLEX TEACHING

HACKING
FLEX TEACHING

10 SOLUTIONS FOR
YOUR BLENDED, HYBRID, OR
DISTANCE LEARNING CLASSROOM

HACK™
Learning
SERIES

HOLLIE
WOODARD

Hacking Flex Teaching
© 2021 by Times 10 Publications

These books are available at special discounts when purchased in quantity for premiums, promotions, fundraising, and educational use. For inquiries and details, contact us at 10Publications.com.

Published by Times 10
Highland Heights, OH
10Publications.com

Cover and Interior Design by Steven Plummer
Editing by Jennifer Zelinger Marshall
Copyediting by Jennifer Jas

Library of Congress Cataloging-in-Publication Data is available.

Paperback ISBN: 978-1-948212-68-7
eBook ISBN: 978-1-948212-70-0
Hardcover ISBN: 978-1-948212-69-4
First Printing: August 2021

For the innovators who refuse to accept the word "can't."

TABLE OF CONTENTS

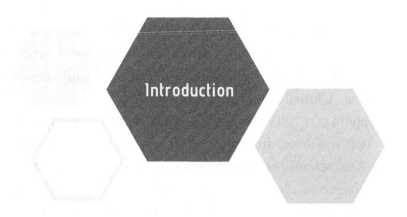

WELCOME TO WONDERLAND

*It's no use going back to yesterday because
I was a different person then.*

—ALICE IN *ALICE'S ADVENTURES IN WONDERLAND*, BY LEWIS CARROLL

M Y FIRST VIRTUAL teaching experience can best be described with one word: panic. It reminded me of a ridiculous game show called *Supermarket Sweep* that I watched as a child. During the final challenge, known as the Big Sweep, the contestants would race around an abandoned grocery store to gather as many items as they could. Though never certain of their objective, I marveled at the panicked way they strategically raced around the store and crossed the finish line to proudly reveal what they had collected, which always seemed like nothing more than crushed chips and dented canned goods.

Using an asynchronous teaching model, I had assigned my students homework with a due date of Monday at midnight, and on

Tuesday morning, I opened a week's worth of work. Like those shoppers, I spent the week panicked, unclear of my objective, and balancing the tasks of learning the technology while developing content. Ultimately, I ended up with lessons that resembled a shopping cart full of broken chips and dented canned goods.

That was seven full years before schools closed the doors on the 2020 school year due to the COVID-19 pandemic. Out of an abundance of caution, the crisis pushed teaching and learning into virtual classrooms and created the biggest educational existential crisis in modern history.

The situation generated multiple problems that had to be solved by technology. It created new educational paradigms, innovated our practice, and exploited the need for digital equity in the form of devices, the internet, and professional development.

Before March 2020, fewer teachers understood the difference between synchronous (occurring at the same time) and asynchronous (not occurring at the same time) teaching, Zoom was simply an onomatopoeia, and teachers greeted their colleagues with "What are you guys doing about Covid in your building?" instead of "How's your year going?" However, solving the problem of educating students while dodging a plague changed the system, resulting in an unprecedented educational update that generated change at a rate that teachers, students, and parents struggled to manage.

Within the first ninety days of pandemic teaching, my district adopted multiple new paradigms, and likely yours did too. They are likely inventing more even now. We began with full-closure asynchronous learning, then full-closure synchronous learning, then partial opening with hybrid A/hybrid B livestream learning, then full opening with hybrid A/hybrid B livestream learning, and finally settled on full-capacity livestream flexible-schedule learning. It is important to note that we sprinkled in some full-closure synchronous learning when our positive COVID-19 numbers surged, and I personally shifted to a month of synchronous learning when I was sick with COVID (#itsnottheflu). For a profession that has not changed its learning model since the Industrial Revolution, all this change and uncertainty was a lot to handle. The term flex teaching was born into existence to describe the resiliency and flexibility that teachers demonstrated during the challenges of pandemic teaching.

Flex teaching is the understanding that education is now fluid, and the educational models created to meet the needs of pandemic teaching and learning are here to stay. It is an awareness that your teaching can no longer be stagnant and redundant with an unbreakable scope and sequence and that student learning depends on your ability to adapt to changing paradigms. Flex teaching is also the understanding that your professional growth, adoption of technology, and twenty-first-century best practices are essential to education's survival.

I always knew that one day, education and technology would merge forces to change the ways we teach and the ways students learn, but before I get to that, I must make a confession:

Technology terrifies me.

Growing up, I took the warnings of my pop culture to heart. I was permanently scarred by Ray Bradbury's warning to never get a virtual reality room because, like the parents in his short story *The Veldt*, you'll end up the main course for a hologram lion in Africa. I'm not 100 percent clear on video's motive for killing the radio star, but I DO know it had something to do with the quick and effortless way in which technology can suck the life

11

out of something once considered super cool and make it completely obsolete. I never quite got over the scene in *War Games* when Matthew Broderick's video game obsession (and inexperience with cyberstalking) brought the Earth just moments away from total annihilation, confirming that the only thing more terrifying than Russia during the Cold War was technology.

During a time when microwaves replaced home-cooked meals, VHS replaced movie theaters, and Atari replaced childhood—I learned to be cautious.

Our local steel mill closed down, confirming my apprehension.

I grew up in Levittown, Pennsylvania, made famous by William Levitt's innovative harnessing of technology and mass production power, resulting in an American Dream oasis known as the suburbs. My father, like my friends' fathers, was a second-generation steelworker and made his living on steel's outsourcing of iron to feed the seemingly unquenchable hunger of the second Industrial Revolution. However, like iron and the radio star, steel was just a dead man walking that would see an end to its heyday.

I was in second grade when I first learned that the steel mill was closing. However, it didn't close down until my senior year in high school.

For that decade, the ebb and flow of the steel industry, and its seemingly unpredictable layoffs, controlled my family's life. During most of that time, I didn't understand the complex world of economics, supply and demand, outsourcing, or automation. What I did know was that sometimes we had electricity, and sometimes we did not. Sometimes we had steak and potatoes for dinner, and sometimes we had chipped beef on toast that my parents called SOS, short for *you know what* on a shingle, which always foreshadowed the impending power outage of my house.

After a decade-long death march, steel—suffering the same fate as its predecessor—finally became an obsolete resource. The steel mill closed, making my father and all the men in my community victims of innovation and technology.

But here's the thing: this didn't happen overnight. It took TEN years for the mill to shut down. That's ten years that my father and the men he worked with could have done something to save themselves. While innovation and technology may have been the cause of death for the mill, it was their own fear that ultimately resulted in their downfall. They didn't want to believe that their industry, like most things, had a life cycle that can only end in one way. They decided their union was strong enough to protect them from the indiscriminate forces of technology and innovation, and they held a false sense of security throughout the most devastating betrayal. Stagnant in the confidence that steel had saved America during World War II and that Americans would always need and want it, they didn't see the vulnerability of their industry. It paralyzed them into a state of business as usual— until there was no business.

When faced with frustration, one instinctually responds in one of three ways: fight, flight, or freeze.

My father froze. For those ten years, he was debilitated by fear as if he were a passenger in a car driven by an uncontrollable force on a dead-end road. When the mill closed, he was broken. He was a man with a lifetime of experience and skills that no longer mattered. As his daughter, consumed with anxiety, I helplessly watched this alchemist with the useless magical power of steelmaking as he was finally forced to innovate himself—but not before suffering the ultimate heartbreak.

Jump forward to the summer of 2008 when I attended my

first edtech graduate class, which immediately reminded me of the unmistakable anxiety about our family's situation during my growing-up years. It was a hybrid graduate course in which I spent eight hours a day for a week in a computer lab with the professor. I worked from home for the next three weeks to complete projects for graduate credit. I wasn't particularly interested in learning about edtech because, as I said, I had a deep-seated fear of technology. However, I needed the credits, and the class was available.

On the first day, the professor, an upbeat, optimistic, and marginally nerdy man, enthusiastically introduced us to wikis, a collaborative website where multiple users can share in the creation and content of the site. He excitedly gave us a lesson design template for a webquest, which is like a digital field trip with tasks to complete at each leg of the journey. He put us into groups and asked us to collaborate on an elementary-level webquest about Colonial America.

As he explained webquests, I felt my chest tighten. I looked around the room to gauge if anyone else was as scared as I was. While some joked that they weren't technologically savvy or were nervous they would make a mistake and break the internet, I had that old foreboding feeling that I was being served *you know what* on a shingle. I couldn't help but feel that this moment foreshadowed the downfall of my industry—education—just like it had crushed my dad's industry.

I raised my hand and said: "Ummm, can you explain to me how you think something like this is good for education?" Confused by my question, he didn't seem to know how to respond. I continued with what I thought was a brilliant analogy. "I don't need Paula Deen in my kitchen if I have her recipe book."

Flushed with embarrassment and with complete earnestness, he asked, "I'm not sure what you mean. Is this Paula person a student of yours?" The class responded with a loud but short-lived laugh.

I pushed back. "Why would I post my lessons online for anyone and everyone to take?"

Now understanding my concern, he said, "Don't think of it as putting your lessons online. Think of it more as providing an alternative learning experience for your students."

Intimidated by the weight of my classmates' stares, I ended my inquisition, but not before aggressively mumbling, "An alternate learning experience led by robots."

Now identified as the classroom alarmist, I reluctantly collaborated with my assigned peers. But I didn't do my best work. I wasn't going to give that up to the internet without a fight.

The reality was that I panicked. My childhood experience taught me that technology ruins everything, and I was terrified to learn that it had made its way into the most sacred of spaces … education.

After spending a week learning new edtech tools and digital instructional strategies that really did make teaching more efficient and improve student learning, I realized that my refusal to use it was not going to make it go away. Acutely aware of what was at stake, I refused to make the same mistakes the mill workers had made and underestimate the power of technology. I would not give technology the upper hand by being naive of the eventual life cycle of education. I would not believe that my union could protect me from the massive innovation that technology forces onto the field. Most importantly, I would not let pride trick me into believing that society's value of teachers would prevent us, as teachers and educational decision-makers, from turning to technology to solve the educational problems that we have yet to solve.

Fearful of its potential, I knew that one day, technology would fully infiltrate education like it had the steel industry.

I had to make a decision. I could fight, flight, or freeze.

I'd already lived through the torturous, unproductive impact of freezing. Flight was not an option for me, as my love for education was too strong. I had no choice left but to fight. I did, however, have a choice in *how* to fight.

I could choose to be the protagonist in *Terminator*, John Connor, who pushes back against the all-consuming power with the ultimate goal of destroying it before it destroys us. Or, I could choose to be the red-pill-enlightened Neo, played by Keanu Reeves, in *The Matrix*. He uses his efforts not to fight for the extinction of technology but to stay in Wonderland and learn as much about it as possible to control it.

I'll take the red pill, please.

Since that class, I've worked to be at the forefront of educational innovation. I finished my grad work with a master's in information technology with an emphasis in utilizing technology. As a high school English teacher in a high-achieving school district in Bucks County, Pennsylvania, I have established myself as an edtech leader. I serve as a volunteer tech coach, piloting multiple edtech-related programs, and serve as an advisor on district technology committees. I've been recognized at the state level as a top educational innovator and have worked on multiple state organizations to advocate for digital equity. I've presented on various edtech topics at state and national conferences, including twenty-first-century best practices, utilization of technology to support special education students, and the functionality of edtech tools. My efforts were recognized by my governor and the department of education when I was identified as a 2022 Pennsylvania Teacher of the Year Finalist.

I mention these experiences not to boost my credentials but to show *how* I chose to fight technology: to learn as much about it as possible so I could control it. Always with a cautious awareness of the power of technology, I use my experience and narrative to help harness technology to guide educational initiatives in my district and state and improve the learning environment for students and teachers.

One of my most successful initiatives, in collaboration with other educators, involved creating a virtual program in my district. In 2013, a full seven years before educators worldwide scrambled to create makeshift online learning plans in the wake of the coronavirus pandemic, I worked with my school administration to launch a virtual English 12 course. It allowed students to take their required twelfth grade English course in a virtual setting. Obsessed with the idea of student choice and developing a platform for students to test their independent learning skills before moving on to college, I enthusiastically embraced the challenges and worked to develop a program that met my students' needs while maximizing their learning. My labor of love has proven to be successful, as it filled a need for our seniors wishing to have a sense of control over their learning. The virtual program has grown to include additional English, social studies, and math classes, resulting in most of my school's seniors electing to take a virtual course.

This experience, while challenging, proved to be incredibly beneficial. It gave me the pedagogy, strategies, and skills to, quite literally, survive pandemic teaching. The majority of my colleagues, through no fault of their own, were not as prepared. The 2020–2021 school year was the most challenging year for educators who, overnight, were forced to adopt new pedagogies and instructional strategies without warning or training.

It reminded me of that familiar anxiety.

If this were a dystopian movie about the existential threat of utilizing technology to solve our educational problems, the 2020–2021 school year would be the flashback scene. In it, we would see frustrated, exhausted, and overwhelmed superintendents, teachers, students, and parents on the brink of giving up on learning. Collectively, they would be sending out the ultimate distress signal: SAVE OUR SCHOOL.

Answering the call, smooth-talking corporate educational software companies with a quick fix, canned lessons, and a for-profit agenda swiftly moved in to seemingly save the day—but not really. As the movie plays out, we learn this moment of weakness and exhaustion results in the demise of teaching and learning.

While that scene can easily be dismissed as a hyperbolic creation out of the imagination of a Level 4 varsity alarmist projecting her childhood trauma onto her life situation, there is no doubt that education has never been more vulnerable. COVID-19 exploited numerous cracks in the glass of education, specifically in areas of equity, that will require multiple solutions. Those solutions will involve technology, and the survival of education will depend on the thoughtful harnessing of technology.

This leaves educators with one of three real options. The first is *flight,* meaning leave the field of education altogether, and, honestly, nobody would blame you, because this is hard.

The second option is *freeze* and allow someone else to use

their experiences and narratives to control the decision-making of your classroom. That didn't work out too well for my dad.

Or ...

The third option is to *fight* by gaining knowledge. You could choose to step into the arena with me and let my virtual teaching experience teach you the "how" of virtual learning and empower you through the most influential period of educational innovation. Like Morpheus teaching Neo the ways of *The Matrix,* I invite you to join the fight and follow me into the wonderland of flex teaching.

Hacking Flex Teaching is divided into ten Hacks to guide you on your journey to become a vibrant teacher who has a virtual curriculum and knows how to use it. As with the other books in the *Hack Learning Series,* each chapter presents easy-to-follow strategies under these section headings: The Problem, The Hack, What You Can Do Tomorrow, A Blueprint for Full Implementation, Overcoming Pushback, and The Hack in Action.

Now, let's go Hack Flex Teaching and engage our online students in authentic learning.

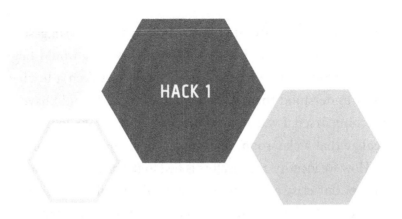

HACK 1

MASTER YOUR LEARNING MANAGEMENT SYSTEM

Build a Digital Classroom

It always seems impossible until it's done.
—NELSON MANDELA

THE PROBLEM: It's hard to create a classroom without an actual classroom

FORTY-SEVEN MINUTES AND twenty-three seconds.

That's the exact amount of time it took for me to decide between a butterfly- or star-themed border for the bulletin board of my very first classroom. I vividly remember sprawling out on the floor of the back corner of Becker's Teacher Supply Store, lost in a sea of colored paper swatches. I was overwhelmed by the daunting power of the bulletin board and the inherent tone it would set for my first classroom. I needed to get it just right for the kids. Butterflies suggested that my classroom would be a place of beautiful transformation, while stars suggested that each of my students had a hidden ability that would begin to shine throughout our time together. I wasn't even a teacher yet, but I understood that the most valuable tool I would have in my teaching arsenal was my classroom. It didn't take long for me to realize that a classroom does much more than create tone.

How we identify as educators is tied to the brilliant form and function of our classroom setting. Are we the tough but warm teacher whose student desks are lined up in perfect rows with inspiring quotes posted across the room? Are we the cool teacher with desks grouped for collaboration with pop culture images and a Funko bobblehead on our desk? Perhaps we are the innovative teacher with flexible seating and bins of Legos easily accessible for kids who need to fidget. Our classrooms serve as expressions of who we are, but they also serve as instructional tools to aid in delivering learning. The way we choose to decorate our classroom allows us to communicate to our students: "This is who I am and who I wish to be for you."

Strategically placed chalkboards, learning centers, morning meeting carpets, and supply carts all serve a purpose in the organization, protocols, and tone of our learning environment. The way we organize our classrooms helps to solve problems before they ever become problems. *You forgot a pencil?* No problem, head on over to the Pencil Rental Station. *You finished your work early?* No problem, head on over to the independent reading beanbag chairs and select a book of your choice. *You are having a difficult time completing your work in the order it was intended?* No problem, simply follow the numbers that have been posted at the station work tables to assist you. We can even complete processes like attendance, bathroom sign-up, and lunch roll call through the creative utilization of our classroom space.

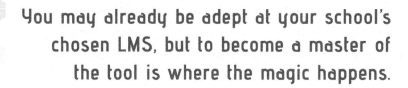

You may already be adept at your school's chosen LMS, but to become a master of the tool is where the magic happens.

1. So, what happens when you can no longer rely on having a classroom?

2. How do we generate the atmosphere of learning that a bulletin board border so effortlessly creates?

3. How do we solve problems before they become problems or handle the everyday processes that were so beautifully executed in our room—without a room?

The answer is to master your LMS. The reality is that a classroom is not a magical space where you become a master wizard of learning just by walking into it. It's just a space. You became the master of your classroom and problem-solved how to use every square inch of the space you were given to provide the best possible learning environment for your students so they could feel safe and supported.

Whether in a classroom or cyberspace, your students still need to feel safe and supported. You will do this by becoming a master of your Learning Management System (LMS).

THE HACK: Master your Learning Management System

You may already be adept at your school's chosen LMS, but to become a master of the tool is where the magic happens. It makes it easier for you to reach a higher level of efficient and effective learning and teaching. An LMS can support classroom, distance, and blended learning. No matter which LMS you are using, your success will depend on your mastery of the system. This begins with developing an understanding and a plan for using the best parts of your LMS that apply to all stakeholders: you, your students, their parents and guardians, and others. Typically, an LMS will help you:

- House and organize your learning artifacts
- Communicate with students and parents
- Provide assessments
- Supply task management tools
- Deliver analytics
- Serve as a gradebook

Mastering these features improves learning, collaboration, communication, and problem-solving. Although it has no walls, a well-designed LMS is a shared virtual space that will create the comfort, organization, and safety of a classroom.

While not all LMSs are created equal, all can be mastered to create a valuable learning space. As you engage with your students in the LMS, remember who benefits the most. While you will spend the most time in the LMS and may have an impulse to organize it in a way that meets your needs, your students' needs and abilities must be at the center of every decision.

WHAT YOU CAN DO TOMORROW

Mastering your LMS is likely not as difficult as you expect, but learning all of the functions will require your commitment and time. Trust me on this: it will be worth it. Here are a handful of ways for you to get started tomorrow.

- **Rely on the LMS help desk**. You can usually access the help desk through your LMS or the application's home website. Most offer a course with several features to help support your learning and development. These include a user's manual, training videos, contact info for tech help, access to community chats where you can connect with other educators using the same LMS, and articles and blogs about their product. You can learn a lot by utilizing the provided resources.

- **Join LMS Facebook Groups**. Facebook has become a great place for teachers from different districts to collaborate and share ideas. By creating or joining an LMS group, teachers can post questions and success stories and problem-solve together, creating a supportive online community to master their LMS. Search the name of your LMS and join a group or several groups. If you can't find one, create your own and push it out to your friends to grow the group.

- **Jump into Professional Learning Networks (PLNs) on Twitter**. A Professional Learning Network is a group of teachers that work together to improve their teaching. Social media is a powerful space for teachers to connect and discuss all things education. If you don't already have a Twitter account, please give it a try. Twitter is an outstanding platform for developing a Professional Learning Network for collaboration. Once you've joined, search your LMS by putting a hashtag (#) in front of the name of your LMS. You will have access to all of the archived tweets about your LMS. In addition, you can begin building a PLN by following the people who tweeted about the LMS. Once you follow them, their tweets will begin filling up your feed. That means every time you access Twitter, you will see the thoughts and ideas of like-minded educators using the same LMS. You can also reach out to them through private messaging for additional collaboration and support.

- **Create a faculty backchannel chat.** A backchannel chat is a private, ongoing conversation that takes place in a virtual space. By accessing a platform like Slack, you can create a backchannel chat for the faculty in your building to post questions, ideas, and success stories. It's difficult for teachers in the same school to find the time to meet and discuss what is and isn't working. The backchannel allows teachers to log in during their prep or free time and collaborate to learn about the LMS.

- **Sign up for professional development.** Reach out to your district's professional development team or tech instructional coaches to sign up for district-sponsored professional development. Districts make an economic investment in the LMS of their choice and often have a budget to teach staff how to utilize it. If none are scheduled, request it.

A BLUEPRINT FOR FULL IMPLEMENTATION

STEP 1: Determine how you will organize learning artifacts.

An LMS will serve as the space where you upload learning artifacts, and students access them. You have options in how you want to organize your artifacts, and your decisions will impact how your students experience their learning. The ease of access will improve their success in the course and decrease the time you will spend answering questions about where the assignment is located. You want to organize the course so it makes sense to the student while decreasing the number of clicks needed to access the learning. Clicks equal time and potential mistakes. As a general rule, choose the path that requires the least number of clicks.

Regardless of how you choose to organize your learning artifacts, discuss the format with your students. Be open to their suggestions by discussing what is working for them and what is not, and adapt to meet their learning needs.

STEP 2: Become familiar with all options for communication.

Spend time understanding the various ways in which your LMS supports communication with students. Use the tools provided by your LMS rather than relying on a secondary resource or external tool, like email, to communicate, as it will take both you and the student out of the program. Think of using external tools to communicate as the equivalent of asking the student to go out into the hallway to talk. You don't want that distraction every time you need to communicate with a student. Use these communication options in the LMS, if possible:

- Instant messaging
- Assignment feedback options
- Content pages
- Group announcements

Equally important, practice using these tools with your students so they can communicate with you when needed and maintain the opportunity for collaboration.

STEP 3: Understand all the available LMS assessment tools.

Mastering assessment tools will improve student learning, and exploring them for your digital classroom is a valuable investment of time. You may get excited about the numerous edtech assessment tools that are on the market; however, it's even better if you can generate effective assessment strategies and tools within your LMS. Try to avoid using external tools that don't easily integrate with your LMS. When you send a student to an external tool, you require them to learn a new skill, redirecting their focus away from the content or skill you are assessing. It will result in additional clicks, which lead to student error. Sending your students unnecessarily to an external tool for assessment is like asking them to go into a different classroom to do their work. You want to allow the student to stay in the class without needing an additional password or username, and the LMS may be able to help.

STEP 4: **Take advantage of the built-in task management tools.**

Task management tools are built-in features such as agendas, calendars, or to-do lists. However, they won't work properly unless the teacher knows how to appropriately create their assignments. When teachers master their LMS, they can use the innate functions to help the students and parents understand what is due. This often takes the form of a calendar or a to-do list that populates on the student's view of the page. Teaching students how to utilize the task management tools will result in higher learning outcomes and decrease the amount of time you spend on emails from confused students and parents about what is due.

STEP 5: **Learn how to access and read your students' course analytics.**

Course analytics are the data that an LMS creates to help you understand your students' work and drive decision-making about instruction. Analytics can provide information about how much time a student has spent on an assignment, which pages they have viewed, and how frequently they access the LMS. These insights are valuable when trying to determine how to meet individual needs. Learning how to access and interpret the analytics will positively impact your instructional decisions.

STEP 6: Learn how to use the grading features in your LMS to generate an easily accessible grade book.

The grade book feature in an LMS is a valuable tool to help your students understand where they stand in the mastery of their work. It can also provide important information for other stakeholders like special education teachers, guidance counselors, and parents who, once given access, can monitor the students' success. In addition, it improves a teacher's efficiency because once they grade an item in the LMS, the score automatically populates in the grade book and calculates the student's grade. It saves the teacher time by skipping the step of inputting grades into the grade book.

Developing mastery of your LMS will create the feel of a classroom, resulting in stronger communication, enhanced efficiency, and higher learning outcomes. When a teacher invests time learning how to master their LMS, they invest in their students' success. A final step in ensuring their success is to provide instruction for the students to *also* become masters of the LMS. We can't assume that students know how to access or master the features to control their learning. Spend time teaching students to master their LMS, and everyone benefits.

OVERCOMING PUSHBACK

Learning Management Systems are incredibly complex, and mastering it will take commitment and dedication. Until you begin to unlock its power and appreciate its efficiency, you may experience the following pushback.

Virtual teaching is just a quick fix for pandemic teaching. Why should I invest in something I won't need to use in the long term? Virtual teaching and learning were here long before the pandemic, and they are here to stay now that administrators, teachers, and parents have experienced its awesome problem-solving potential. Schools will continue to explore virtual teaching and learning, specifically to improve the areas of equity and access. Choosing to invest in learning your district's LMS will pay off as you can depend on it to help solve educational problems.

I have so much to do. How can I invest time and effort into learning LMS functions? Whether you are teaching face-to-face, hybrid, or distance learning, an LMS can positively impact your teaching. In the beginning, you will have to invest time and effort. However, mastering it will pay off in dividends as you will get a major return on your investment. Imagine never having to waste your morning making copies, carrying home a bag full of papers to grade, or responding to a parent request about missing work. An LMS empowers teachers, students, and parents by changing the way everyone experiences school. It's well worth the investment of your time.

THE HACK IN ACTION

I've been working in my district's selected LMS, Canvas, for eight years. Each year, my mastery improves as I've worked hard to understand how to use the program to manage the learning in my classes. As a result, it has become my virtual classroom and serves as the shared space where my students and I can meet to conduct the business of learning.

When it comes to storing and organizing my learning artifacts, presenting the information to my students in an agenda format has been the most productive. My students have been provided with school-issued assignment books since elementary school, so organizing their learning into weekly modules and separating the daily assignments has been the best way to present my lessons to my students.

Week 12 October 19-23	
MONDAY	
10-19 Agenda	
ASP Discussion Questions	Oct 19 10 pts
TUESDAY	
10-20 Agenda	
Ch. 1 A Separate Peace Reading	Oct 20 25 pts
WEDNESDAY	
10-21 Agenda	
Ch. 1 Reading Quiz	Oct 21 10 pts
THURSDAY	
10-22 Agenda	
Ch. 1 Written Analysis Oct	Oct 22 10 pts
FRIDAY	
10-23 Agenda	
Ch. 1 Summary/Summary	Oct 23 20 pts

Image 1.1: In this sample, students simply have to click on the module week and then read through the module to access the day's agenda and assignment.

In addition, I use the communication tools in Canvas to communicate with my students when working synchronously or asynchronously. I also use Canvas to help me with both my formative and summative assessments. Although I could send my students out of Canvas to access other edtech tools, it usually doesn't make sense for them to leave our LMS and go to another site, requiring another login and password, when Canvas offers the assessment capabilities. By using the task management tools in Canvas, I am solving numerous problems for my students. Fewer obstacles equals greater outcomes.

It took me a while to figure out how to appropriately create assignments so they would show up as tasks for students to complete. Now that I know how to do it, the LMS automatically generates a calendar so the student can see what is due and access the assignment by clicking directly on it. In addition, when it is complete, it is crossed-off, showing the student what work they completed. It's a valuable use of my LMS, but it took me some work to master how to use it appropriately. Once I did, I stopped getting emails from confused students and their parents about what was due and when.

14	15	16
~~Vocabulary 9 Assignments~~	SUBMIT RESEARCH PAPER HERE	AL-(GG Intro) Importance of Historical Context
		AL-(GG Intro) 100 Years of Equal Rights
		AL-(GG Intro) Story of an Hour
		College and Career Readiness Eleventh Grade English

Image 1.2: This is a sample of the task management calendar in Canvas.

Analytics are an interesting component of an LMS. They can tell you which pages your students accessed and for how long. This feature has proven valuable when determining why work hasn't been completed or to help me out with my pacing. I've had students message me that they could not complete the assignment because they didn't understand part of it, and then their analytics show that they never clicked on the page. That is always a fun email to send, complete with a screenshot that shows that they never clicked on it. I only have to send that email once before the students send out a massive group text that I can see their clicks on the site. This has helped me make planning decisions, as I can see how long it takes my students to complete assignments. It provides valuable data that makes my students' learning needs visible.

Finally, it took me a few years to fully commit to the grade book in Canvas, but when I did, I regretted not doing it sooner. My email used to be filled with questions about student grades. However, now I use the Canvas grade book as my primary record of student achievement. I no longer have to spend time fielding questions about assessments. Because all my assignments are recorded through Canvas, students simply click on their grade book and can see their average and whether I have completed grading something. Once I assess an assignment in Canvas, it automatically appears as a graded assignment in the grade book, with most students receiving notifications on their Canvas app that their work has been assessed.

As a high school teacher, it is easy for me to encourage other teachers to turn their LMS into their digital classroom because I have older students who have mastered independent learning. But this Hack works for all grade levels. Here's how a kindergarten teacher used their LMS to create a virtual classroom for their young students.

Ryan Berger is a kindergarten and STEM teacher who has been

recognized as a top educational innovator, a Teacher of the Year as named by *Philadelphia Magazine*, and a popular conference presenter. When the pandemic sent students home for online learning, kindergarten teachers had an especially daunting task.

Berger, however, mastered his LMS, Seesaw, which allowed him to solve the problems associated with virtual learning while empowering his young learners.

Berger likes Seesaw because he can organize all of his learning artifacts and activities in one location. Students, parents, and teachers know where everything is located and can always refer back to activities completed throughout the year. He uses Seesaw's scheduling feature to set up activities in advance and differentiate student work.

"A teacher can assign an activity to the entire class, some students, or specific students and can schedule the activity to appear on a specific date and time. When activities are assigned to students, it automatically goes under the 'to-do list' in the activities section of Seesaw. All assignments will stay there until they are completed. Once the students complete an assignment, it automatically moves to the 'done' section."

This alerts him that he has an assignment to approve, but it also allows parents to know exactly what task their child has left to complete. Using the task management tools and teaching his students and parents how to access them have generated independence in his students and empowered his parents to provide support from home.

Berger's mastery of the communication tools in Seesaw has created a dynamic space for him to communicate with his students and their parents. One way is by providing directions for an assignment.

"When a teacher is creating an assignment, they are able to provide written directions with Seesaw-specific icons, as well as provide recorded verbal instructions for the activity."

Berger acknowledges that his students need more support than simply understanding the directions. Because of his students' undeveloped reading skills, he needs the LMS to read problems to the students.

"You also have the ability to leave up to twenty voice notes on a page in Seesaw. Any image, shape, or text box can be linked to audio so that students can click on the speaker icon and listen to the directions, or have the question read aloud to them. For example, when creating a math assignment, I could write out the word problem at the top of the page, but then link audio to the word problem that reads the question to the students."

In addition, Berger has learned that he can silently communicate to his students which tools they will use for the activity by selecting specific icons when he writes the directions. Finally, he uses the messaging system to send messages to parents, students, or the class. He uses this feature to remind them of events, assignments, or materials they might need for an activity.

As a kindergarten teacher, Berger doesn't use grades to communicate student success. Instead, he collaborates with parents on the skills their children are developing. He has mastered his LMS to make this collaboration with parents easy and efficient. On Back-to-School Night, he has his parents sign up and connect to their child's account, giving them access to their child's Seesaw portfolio. Parents have access to their child's work and anything their child has been tagged in. A teacher could take a photo or video and send it out to the entire class or a specific student. Any student who is tagged in a photo, video, or assignment automatically gives their parents access to their work. The teacher can allow parents to leave comments on student work as well. When students complete assignments or the teacher posts photos or videos, the parents receive a push notification on their phones. Parents can see exactly what their child was doing in school that day. The parents can leave a text or audio message for their child, and the child can also leave a message for their parents. Berger loves this positive impact on student learning.

"The parent communication in Seesaw is a window into my classroom. Seesaw allows the parents to see what their child was doing that day through videos, photos, and assignments, which leads to conversations at home. I've had many parents tell me that they loved that feature because they knew exactly what was happening in the class."

By mastering his LMS, Berger has created a digital classroom space that encourages independence, communication, and collaboration. As kindergarten students, they require a ton of support because they are just beginning their learning journey. However, with his investment in learning how to master the tools, he has figured out how to solve the problems associated with their learning needs and create a virtual classroom in which students feel safe and supported.

While it may not have a powerful star or butterfly theme, a learning management system is a tool that does just what its name says—it manages learning. When used properly, it can transcend traditional education by providing a one-stop shopping experience for teaching and learning. By mastering it, teachers can gain efficiency around their learning artifacts, communication, assessments, task management, analytics, and grading. Whether you are teaching seniors or kindergartners, in person or through distance learning, a mastered LMS can become a digital safe space for student learning that can replace or augment the form and function of your classroom.

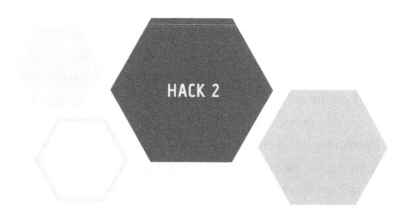

COMMUNICATE CONSISTENTLY

Set Up Norms, Templates, Routines, and Protocols

*The single biggest problem in communication
is the illusion that it has taken place.*
—GEORGE BERNARD SHAW

THE PROBLEM: Teachers struggle to communicate well in a virtual setting

IT'S NOT YOU; it's me. We've all seen this narrative play out in television shows and movies, where two well-intentioned and likable characters agree to go their separate ways. Out of respect and, arguably, love, they choose to nobly blame themself for their inadequacies instead of blaming their partner for some unfixable character flaw.

When it came to the problems with my virtual learning communication, however, the problem was me. In my first year of virtual teaching, I reluctantly learned that the burden for successful communication, especially in a virtual learning setting, lies squarely on me, the classroom teacher.

I certainly did not feel this way at first. I thought the hardest part would be in starting the program. I had no idea that the hardest part would be in answering the unending steady stream of emails—morning, noon, and night—that I would receive from students who were confused about what to do, when to do it, and how to do it. The frustrating part was that I had clearly articulated ALL of those answers in the directions. They simply had to click and learn! To make it even worse, I would repeatedly answer the same questions. I became resentful of the emails, the questions, and the kids because of what felt like constant nagging. Everything they needed to know was right there.

I would spend my weekends meticulously planning my lessons and writing out directions. Each week, I would think, "This is it ... no way anyone could be confused." With full confidence, I would post the assignment and hit publish, and within minutes, my laptop would ding with notifications from confused kids who needed more from me. I secretly accused them of laziness instead of rationalizing that if they were lazy, they wouldn't be emailing me to advocate for clarity. I would yell out privately in frustration, "What is wrong with these kids?"

Streamlining your communication processes is like gifting yourself more time on the clock.

The answer was, of course, that nothing was wrong with these kids. But something was wrong with my communication. The emails were not a representation of a failure by the kids. It was the opposite: the kids were demonstrating grit and resilience in advocating for their learning needs. These were qualities that, ironically, I had hoped they would develop by taking my virtual course. The emails simply represented my failure to communicate properly. It wasn't them; it was me.

THE HACK: Communicate consistently

All successful relationships have one thing in common—good communication. It's in the natural communication ebb and flow between students and teachers where the magic of learning occurs. But that ebb and flow is compromised in a virtual learning environment. The absence of face-to-face time, where teachers and students easily and naturally engage, can negatively impact the way students and teachers feel about one another.

Whether it is giving directions, providing feedback, generating motivation, or offering encouragement, teachers must be consistent and intentional about their online communication. When they are, they can still develop successful relationships that are necessary to cultivate learning. Hacking these four communication paths is especially critical in virtual learning environments. They are:

- Your communication to the class

- Your communication to a student

- A student's communication to you

- A student's communication with the class

By using templates, protocols, and routines to communicate consistently, teachers can hack their communication needs and those of their students, and they can reclaim their email.

WHAT YOU CAN DO TOMORROW

Streamlining your communication processes is like gifting yourself more time on the clock. Here are ways to get started.

- **Create a class agenda template.** Students like to know what to expect when class begins. Don't we all? Meet their needs and make it easy on yourself by creating a simple class agenda template and adjusting the details for each class. Use any format you like for this teacher-to-student communication tool, but you'll want to at least match the needs of your students and fit your personality. Image 2.1 shows an example of a daily class agenda I've used with my high school students.

  I begin each day with the following items on each class agenda:

  - **Humor:** Lead with a humorous meme, gif, or inside joke.
  - **Praise:** Provide some sort of whole-class praise.
  - **Objective:** Share a sentence that explains my objective for the class.

- **Directions:** Chunk and number the directions so students can understand how many actions they will need to take during the class period.

Great job completing your first essay this school year! I was impressed that everyone submitted it on time and remembered to have a Works Cited page! Well done!

Today we are going to switch gears and begin to analyze the importance of historical context when analyzing literature.

1. Please read the article and answer all of the questions on the assignment titled: *Importance of Historical Context*.

2. Please read the article *100 Years of Equal Rights* and provide a written response to the prompt posted in the assignment text box.

3. Please begin reading *The Story of an Hour* by Kate Chopin.

You won't have enough time to finish this in class, but you will be provided time tomorrow to finish.

Image 2.1: A sample daily agenda.

- **Add audio or video instructions**. Depending on the age and literacy of your students, you may want to include recorded audio or video instead of written directions. A best practice is to chunk your audio and video into each specific step you would like the students to complete. So instead of posting a five-minute video detailing all the items your students must do, break up the video into smaller chunks based on each step of the directions. For example, let students know that you've shared five videos, so there are five activities to complete. This will support students with under-developed executive functioning by communicating to them at each step.

- **Identify your top communication tool and teach students how to use it**. Identify which communication tools you will use for individual communication between you and your students, as well as parents and guardians. Create a quick lesson to help your students learn how to use the tool. It doesn't need to be fancy. Post the lesson in a place that students can access throughout the school year when they need help communicating with you.

- **Model best practices when sending messages or emails**. Many students have not been taught how to properly send an email or message. This is a valuable digital literacy skill that you can teach them. Providing direct instruction on this skill will show students the importance of email writing and encourage them to engage with you. Too many students feel that emailing or messaging a teacher is a nuisance and don't want to bother us. However, when you let them know your preferred channel, you give them permission to reach out to you when needed.

- **Start a slow chat**. Develop a lesson that includes a slow chat to cultivate student-to-class communication. A slow chat consists of:

  1. Posting a question in a discussion board tool
  2. Providing a specific amount of time to answer the question
  3. Giving directions for responding to their classmates' posts

  In asynchronous instruction, start by posting one to three questions a week and give your students a couple of days to make their initial response. Then, give them a few more days to follow the directions and respond to their classmates' thoughts and ideas.

  In a synchronous class, shorten the amount of time they have to complete the task. Try posting the question using the discussion tool in your LMS, then give them four minutes to respond to the question and read their classmates' responses. Provide directions on how they should acknowledge their classmates' responses. It could be as simple as: "Read your classmates' responses and like the ones that are similar to yours" or "Find the responses that are different from yours and type 'That's new to me' in the chatbot." After the time is up, quickly scroll through and find the responses that have been most liked or commented on, and ask the students to elaborate on their thinking and share with the class, either by speaking or typing.

A slow chat type of structured routine creates the opportunity for all students to connect with their peers, allowing them to use their voice, be heard, and feel acknowledged for their thinking.

- **Model the format of the slow chat.** Create a low-stakes topic in which the lesson objective is to learn how to navigate the slow chat, as opposed to obtaining mastery of the topic you are discussing. Allow the students to focus on learning the format without worrying about being assessed on their comments.

A BLUEPRINT FOR FULL IMPLEMENTATION

STEP 1: Put communication templates to work.

Create a digital template for your communication to the whole class. Include the who, what, where, when, and why of the class. Using a consistent format will save you time and help your students know that they can rely on you to communicate in a certain way. This reduces their anxiety about the unknowns and cuts back on their barrage of questions directed to you.

STEP 2: Create communication routines.

Communicating with individual students can be challenging in a virtual learning setting; just because a message is sent does not mean it is received. Depending on which method you use to communicate with individual students, you'll want to work a daily routine into your course so students begin to expect a message from you. Some students quickly understand and demonstrate the responsibility of checking their messages daily and will not need to be prompted. However, younger students or those with executive functioning issues may need to be prompted to check for messages from you.

When I communicate with individual students, I use the communication tools within my LMS. They function like an email or direct message when students are logged in. During blended or synchronous instruction, I require all students to log in to the LMS before we even review the day's agenda. They record their attendance in the LMS via an attendance quiz. After completing the quiz, I prompt all students to check their inbox to see if they received a message from me. Then, I provide class time for them to access the message and respond in a message back to me. When I'm establishing this routine, it takes a little longer because I have to walk the students through how to access the message and, of course, how to respond. However, once they establish the routine, they quickly and efficiently receive and then respond to my messages. I always end every message with the line: "Please write back so I know you read it." This is important because sometimes my message doesn't require them to do anything. Having them signal back is a great way to verify that they received it.

For asynchronous instruction, I also use the communication tools within the LMS; however, I use a quiz, similar to the attendance quiz, to remind them to check their messages. The quiz has a true-or-false question that states: "I checked my inbox for a message from Mrs. Woodard." The quiz serves as a reminder to check for messages, and I can look at the results to see whether the student checked their inbox.

STEP 3: Design student communication protocols.

Scroll through your emails, identify repeated areas or subjects that take too much of your time or emotions to problem-solve, and then create a protocol to mainstream the process. You know it can be overwhelming and even emotionally draining when your email buzzes with a steady stream of student questions, requests, and bits of information that need responses. However, when you design protocols for the most common communication needs, specifically those that require problem-solving, it will help you streamline the process. Start by identifying the mode of communication you would like your students to use when reaching out to you, such as email, text, or the direct message feature in your LMS. Next, identify the type of request that you get emailed about the most, and create a specific protocol for students to follow when they have that type of request. Spend class time going over the protocol and creating a sample correspondence so students will understand your expectations. Post the protocol where students will be able to access it throughout the year.

I ask students to communicate with me through the LMS. I provide a sample email message for the students to follow when messaging me, and it includes the subject line, greeting, body of the email, and closing. I also discuss the importance of tone, speaking for oneself, being specific, and stating whether they would like me to write back to them. We then use class time to practice this skill. In addition, I explain that if they do not hear from me within twenty-four hours of their email, they should resend it because an error occurred—either with the system or with me.

I believe in the value of establishing protocols for recurring issues, as a lot of the communication I receive from students is about requesting help for technical difficulties. Things will go wrong. Actually, many things will go wrong. You will forget to post something, assign the wrong due date, accidentally hyperlink the wrong site, or any number of things that you can mess up. Students will lose Wi-Fi, get an error message, be unable to download the file, or you name it. You have your own mental list of things that have gone awry.

Before I developed a protocol, I was overwhelmed and was looking to assign blame. If a student emailed me that something was going wrong, I often jumped to the conclusion that the student was trying to get out of the work. I'm not sure why that was my go-to thought, but unfortunately, it was. I wasn't much easier on myself. If they pointed out that I had made a mistake, it felt like they were emailing to tell me I was the worst teacher on the planet and should look for work in a field that required less technical skill. The reality is that none of this was true. The truth was that there was a technical difficulty: nothing more and nothing less.

So, I created an unemotional and nonjudgmental protocol to help deal with the yucky awkwardness of mistakes. I simply tell the students that if something goes wrong, they have to follow this process:

1. Take a screenshot.

2. Attach it to an email or message, detailing what you were doing and what went wrong.

3. Send the email to me BEFORE the assignment is due.

4. Wait for my response and then follow the directions in the response email.

5. Communicate back to me, stating that the problem has or has not been corrected.

6. If the problem cannot be corrected through email, you will receive an extension. You must see the words "you have an extension" to be excused.

Creating these steps normalized the fact that technical difficulties happen and gave everyone an unemotional and fearless protocol that doesn't turn into a power struggle or digital standoff. It also drastically decreased the number of back-and-forth emails required to assess and fix the difficulty.

STEP 4: Build structured class communication routines.

The most challenging communication to achieve in virtual learning is student-to-class communication. It's critically important to provide opportunities for students to use their voice in education, yet the nature of virtual learning negatively impacts authentic student-to-student communication. Asynchronous learning obviously makes communication more difficult when students are not in the lesson at the same time. However, synchronous lessons have their own obstacles, as unmuting the microphone to speak creates an odd delay that often makes students not even want to participate in discussions. Create weekly and daily routines for cultivating student-to-student communication.

OVERCOMING PUSHBACK

It still surprises me when teachers say they don't have time to communicate well and then wonder why their relationships are strained and their students are confused. Here are a couple of common excuses around digital communication and how to solve them.

I want communication to be natural. Communication is a natural process, and designing templates, routines, and protocols is necessary to standardize what normally comes naturally. It is true that when we interact in person in the same space at the same time, we have the benefits of body language and peer modeling. When we must communicate virtually, we have to work a bit harder to model and define good communication for our students. While it may feel forced and unnatural at first, it gets easier (and less awkward) with time. Your students will look to you for an example, so model clear, positive communication. Before long, it will become the natural social norm of your class.

With everything I am responsible for in the class, communication seems like an added burden. Teachers are not only responsible for teaching a subject; they are preparing young minds for the future and giving students a launching pad for life. Communication skills are a critical component of your curriculum, and students often learn this skill through modeling. In a physical classroom, students develop verbal communication skills through thousands of interactions and immediate feedback, both positive and negative, that validates their efforts.

When the setting changes to virtual, students are at a disadvantage. For example, they may lack:

- Experience with virtual interactions
- Literacy skills that impact their ability to read and understand what is expected of them, and written expression skills to properly articulate their questions or concerns
- Executive functioning skills to process the information and execute what is being asked of them

When you take full responsibility for the communication in your class, it creates better learning outcomes and stronger relationships. It sets an example that students can carry with them into their future. It also helps ensure that you are not discriminating against students who may not have the skill set or ability to communicate in a virtual setting.

THE HACK IN ACTION

A high-frequency issue I discovered in virtual teaching is the extension requests from my high school students for late or missing work.

When I took on teaching remotely, I wanted to provide students with the opportunity to practice being independent learners. I also knew it would require a certain level of patience and grace that I don't typically afford students in face-to-face classrooms. Primarily, students would be responsible for managing their time and task completion. They would no longer have the benefit of a teacher telling them exactly what to do and when to do it like they do in person. Instead, they would be required to assess the assigned work, determine how long they thought it would take them to complete it all, develop a schedule to get it done—and then actually complete it.

It turns out that these were not skills that most of my students had developed—even though they were seniors—and they made mistakes. All of them had the best intentions to complete their work, but they quickly learned that the time it takes to complete the tasks could easily get away from them. They overestimated how much time they would have over the weekend or underestimated how much time it would take to read a chapter on their own. Regardless of the reason, late and missing work became huge issues in virtual learning.

Without a policy or process, I would be placed in the uncomfortable position of being judge and jury. Essentially, I would have to assess each individual case and determine if they deserved an extension with or without penalty. This was emotionally exhausting and took away my focus on the actual teaching of the course. So, I determined it was best to support student learning in a nonpunitive way so they could work to develop this critical skill and learn the content I was responsible for teaching.

I created another protocol that would grant extensions if they met the following criteria:

1. Email me before the assignment is due to request an extension.

2. Clearly articulate the name of the assignment.

3. Tell me when you would like the assignment to be due.

Notice, I don't ask them why it is late. As a rule, if they follow this process before the assignment is due, there is no penalty or grade reduction for lateness. You may likely be wondering if students take advantage of this, and I'll be honest: they don't. The reality is that life happens, mistakes get made, and all I care about is whether the student learned what I'm trying to teach them. More importantly, this protocol has decreased the number of emails I get from panicked students (trying to convince me that they are worthy of my forgiveness), unnecessarily chewing up my time and my emotions.

When establishing these protocols with my students, I provide a screencast video to explain the steps, accompanied by written directions. It is permanently posted in my LMS so they can access it when needed. I also assess their understanding of the process with a formative assessment and a sample correspondence. If I do happen to receive a message that is not following the protocol, I simply reply, "Please refer to our class protocol," and I hyperlink the page where I posted it.

Communication routines create a structure that promotes student engagement. In my digital classrooms, these structures have increased student involvement in group discussions. For example, I have developed the weekly routine of facilitating slow chats for my asynchronous and synchronous classes. (See the description of slow chats earlier in this chapter.)

Liz Potash is a health and physical education teacher from my district, and I taught her how to use the slow chat to improve her health class discussion. Liz is a passionate and innovative health and physical education advocate who has presented at the state level. She said, "Integrating twenty-first-century best practices into my curriculum has been challenging because many think of phys ed and technology and get a vision of kids running on the track holding Chromebooks. That's not exactly what we do, but with the help of a motivated department, we've been able to create a blended environment in both health and phys ed."

Despite being well-versed in the utilization of technology, Liz was blindsided by the total school shutdown as a result of COVID-19. She was particularly concerned about her health classes. Given the trauma of the pandemic, she knew that health could be a safe place for students to explore their emotions, as learning about mental health and trauma is an essential pillar of the curriculum. Liz figured out almost immediately that the nature of virtual learning makes it difficult to create an environment conducive to authentic class discussions like her face-to-face classroom afforded. She found that her time-tested, face-to-face strategies to engage students in class discussions fell flat in the virtual setting.

"The students at home are very hesitant to participate in class discussions during virtual synchronous instruction. Generally, in school, we are able to have class discussions, but it is very difficult discussing such personal topics without physical interaction." The students' lack of participation in the virtual environment was impacting their learning.

Liz reached out to me for help on how to improve her student-to-class communication, and I introduced her to the slow chat. She said, "I presented the students with three different controversial topics related to drug laws, and we used the discussion board in live time on Canvas to converse. The slow chat was able to get my entire class having a 'discussion.' By asking the students to not only post their responses but also comment to each other back and forth, the students had an actual dialogue."

Recreational Marijuana in New Jersey Discussion

Facts:

- On Nov. 16, 2020, the New Jersey Senate passed S.2535/A.1897, which would legalize possession of up to six ounces of cannabis. The bill also contains expungement provisions and removes penalties related to marijuana use.
- The bill allows people 21 and older to use marijuana without a doctor's approval. The amendment directs the legislature and regulators to set up a market to grow, distribute, and tax the product.
- Under the ballot initiative, marijuana products will be subject to the state's 6.625% sales tax. The legislature could also authorize local governments to collect an additional 2% sales tax on cannabis, and it is considering imposing an excise tax on cultivation.

1. Post in the discussion why you agree/disagree with the legislation.

2. Respectfully comment on 3 classmates' posts:

   - Do you agree/disagree with their stance? Why/why not?
   - Do you have a question about their comment?
   - Did your classmate make a point that you hadn't considered?

3. Go back to your original post and read the replies.

Image 2.2: An example of a slow chat discussion assignment using the LMS discussion board feature.

Liz was pleased with the results and has utilized this communication routine to tackle other sensitive topics like mental health and abusive relationships. She credits the success of the activity to the time it allows students to develop their answers.

"The slow chat gives students time to process their thoughts before posting a response and then time to process further when commenting to each other. Most students seem to be more comfortable conversing digitally, so the format really encourages great conversation."

Having a consistent routine that provides the time and space to communicate, rather than trying to host a live virtual class discussion that is vulnerable to feeling stagnant and forced, is the key to thoughtful, respectful, and productive communication in a virtual learning setting.

By creating consistent communication, teachers take full responsibility for their interactions with students collectively and individually and for the students' communication with the teacher and their classmates. While communication is more of a challenge in a virtual setting, there are ways to overcome the obstacles and make it feel as natural as possible. By creating norms through templates, routines, and protocols, teachers can build a system of support to help students develop the soft skills of virtual communication that they will use for the rest of their lives.

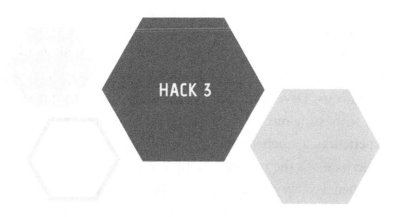

EMBED ENGAGEMENT

Design Engaging Activities, Gamifications, and Celebrations

Never, ever underestimate the importance of having fun.
—RANDY PAUSCH

THE PROBLEM: Teachers need help engaging students through a screen

IF YOU'VE TAUGHT a virtual class, think back to your earliest sessions. Perhaps they can best be summed up by one of two songs: "Is There Anybody Out There?" by Pink Floyd or "Sabotage" by the Beastie Boys. To put it simply, it can feel like alienation or complete chaos. Whether you are a cameras-on, cameras-off, or your-choice classroom, engaging with students across the internet is arguably one of the more challenging and frustrating experiences for teachers adapting to virtual learning.

Developing relationships with our students is a fundamental component of effective teaching. Not only does it allow us to do a better job of teaching our students, but it also serves a purpose for us. Developing positive relationships with our students and witnessing our impact on them is one of the most satisfying experiences a teacher can have. Despite being overworked and underpaid, it's the reason we return each fall.

When I surveyed staff to see what areas of support I could provide for them, ideas for engagement became the number one ask. One colleague said, "How can I teach them if I don't even know them?" Another said, "Unless I'm teaching and mute them, it's a total free-for-all because they don't care about me because they don't know me." Yet another colleague, frustrated by a no-cameras-on mandate, exclaimed, "I've been teaching them for five months, and I don't even know what they look like!"

In the unnatural setting of an online "classroom," especially if your school has adopted a cameras-off or choice philosophy, teachers find it difficult to release their usual super cool teacher persona. Jokes that usually score a ten in the classroom fall flat in the awkwardness of the dark screen and muted microphones, leaving many teachers unwilling to even try the next joke in their arsenal, fearful they will get the same reaction … or lack of a reaction.

The awkwardness is not exclusive to teachers, as students have articulated their discomfort in an online classroom. For students who have to endure a cameras-on mandate, they may feel like their teacher and classmates are intrusively entering their home. One student described the cameras-on mandate in the following way:

"Imagine, a teacher asks you to pull your desk up to the front of the room and turn it around to face the entire class. Then, they proceed to go on with their teaching as the entire class stares at you while you take your notes and do your work."

Not a single teacher worth their merit would ask a kid to endure that type of unwanted attention and humiliation, and yet, that is what some of our students in a cameras-on setting endure. To make it worse, their classmates now get to see whether their bedroom, living room, or some other room in their house looks cool or uncool.

Unfortunately, due to synchronous live-streamed classes and the awkwardness that exists for the teacher and the students, the relationships feel strained. The natural, in-person banter—that magically builds relationships, trust, and a safe environment conducive for learning—is missing. Because of this disconnect, it is more important than ever to connect with your students. But you'll want to change how you go about it.

THE HACK: Embed engagement

Teachers can be intentional with their engagement by embedding activities, gamifications, and celebrations into their lesson plans. These are instructional strategies with the objective of increasing student engagement. In a face-to-face setting, teachers may feel uncomfortable taking instructional time to play a non-content-related game or have an off-topic discussion. They wouldn't want to be accused of being unprofessional or off-task. Of course, they end up using the natural breaks built into the school day, like the time before the bell rings, the last few minutes of class when the work has been done, and hallway encounters, to get to know their students and engage them in the learning.

Since these natural occurrences don't take place in a virtual learning setting, teachers must find ways to embed engagement by creating and using class time to implement activities, gamifications, and celebrations. Engaging your students leads to better relationships and better learning outcomes.

WHAT **YOU** CAN DO TOMORROW

While it takes time and trust to build student engagement, start small, and the momentum will build. Think about these quick strategies today and choose one or two to begin tomorrow.

- **Make space for student voice and choice**. Develop an assignment that you can turn into a daily activity that cultivates student voice and choice. Based on the theme of your unit, design a quick, creative lesson that allows your students to express their opinions or skills. Give them an opportunity to share during the class, whether out loud or via a slide, a presentation, or typed answers.

- **Copy good gamification ideas**. Teachers love to share what works, and they know what goes around, comes around. There's often no need to create something brand new unless you have the inspiration and energy. For now, go to Twitter and search #gamification for ideas on how to gamify your lessons and to connect with teachers who are innovating in that area. Gamification can be intimidating, but you don't have to do it alone. Numerous professionals create and share great templates that can give you everything you need to add a gamification component to your lessons tomorrow.

- **Ask, and you shall receive**. Develop an engagement committee or party planning committee with your students to brainstorm ways to increase student engagement in your course. Students want the class to be fun, and if you are having a difficult time getting them engaged in the class, ask them for help. Volunteers might agree to meet you online after school to brainstorm ideas for future class activities or parties. They have already likely thought of a thousand ways to make your class more enjoyable, and by asking for their ideas, the only thing you stand to lose is disengagement.

- **Find out what they're passionate about.** Create a quick student interest survey to learn more about your students. What are they passionate about? What do they collect? Where do they work? What are their talents? What do they do in their spare time? What do they read? What sports do they play? Do they perform? What are their families like? Use what you learn from the survey to embed their interests into your lessons.

A BLUEPRINT FOR FULL IMPLEMENTATION

STEP 1: Start class with a burst of engagement.

A synchronous class has the benefit of having students participate in real time; however, getting students to participate can be challenging. Just like in a face-to-face classroom, the first ten minutes of the class can set the tone for the rest of the period. Create an opening activity that encourages students to unmute and join in an authentic and natural discussion to create an energy of engagement that can last throughout the period.

One idea to build engagement into every online class is through daily student participation in a SlideShow Share. Assign the project to everyone and select one student to share each day near the beginning of class. The assignment involves posing a question that loosely relates to the class curriculum or theme and asking each student to create a slide that answers the question and includes visuals, and to be prepared to share the slide and discuss its contents with the class.

For example, in my film studies class, I asked the students to select three movies they would like to see added to the curriculum. Their assignment was to decorate the slide with images of the films and write up a short response as to why the films should be adopted into the course. Then, for the next thirty days—because that's my class size—I selected students to present their slides to the class and discuss their choices.

Each student's SlideShow Share presentation goes down like this:

1. The student shares their slide and makes their pitch.

2. The class engages in a discussion about the movies.

3. I post a quick poll through my streaming service, and students vote on which film they would add to the curriculum.

4. I officially add the film with the most votes to "Mrs. Woodard's Period 9 Critical Viewing Class Curriculum," which they know is an honorary designation only because we have no power to change the curriculum. However, it buys me five minutes

of authentic student-led discussion and gives me
valuable insight into who these students are behind
that muted mic and darkened screen.

You can readily adapt the SlideShow Share activity for any
topic, format, grade level, or subject. You can use it to kick things
off with a burst of engagement at the beginning of class or within
the lesson as a type of gamification.

STEP 2: Add a gamification component.

Who doesn't like a game? Add the classic elements of game-
playing and competition to an assignment with the objective of
increasing engagement and improving learning outcomes.

For example, in preparation for an upcoming unit on *The Great
Gatsby*, I used the SlideShow Share activity to explore the theme
of love in a Love Song Battle. I asked students to find the ultimate
love song and create a slide to share. On the slide, they identified
the name and year of the song, provided a thirty-second clip of
the song, and created a write-up as to why it is the ultimate love
song. I asked two students to share their songs each day. After the
students presented their clips and delivered a one-minute pitch
as to why their song is the ultimate love song, the class selected
the winner through a class poll. The winning song was moved
into the final round of the top ten love songs. I created an online
poll that the students shared on their social media, allowing their
peers to vote for the Ultimate Love Song. The simple gamification of the activity immediately and electrically increased engagement, as the presenters came alive knowing they had to convince
their classmates to vote. Their classmates' engagement was pal-
pable as they provided commentary to hype up the competition.

Start with one activity, gamified lesson, or celebration, and notice the difference in the energy of your class.

For more virtual-setting gamification activities, such as a "math problem zombie apocalypse survival game" and "the class is lava" game, see the Hack in Action section of this chapter.

STEP 3: Look for opportunities to celebrate.

Whether it's celebrating the class mastery of a complex concept, perfect attendance, or everyone turning their cameras on, look for opportunities to celebrate with your students. Sticker charts, gif dance parties, and virtual confetti cannons can mark a celebration and make it fun to be in your class, whether in person, remote, or a mix of both. Feel free to be bold and go all-in on a celebration. Nothing brings a class together more quickly than a good old-fashioned class party. Just because you aren't in the same physical space doesn't mean you can't celebrate together in a virtual space.

In my in-person classroom, I look for reasons to celebrate and build classroom community. Parties allow students and teachers to step away from the constant demands of teaching and learning and instead just enjoy each other's presence and the time to celebrate. Here are two virtual celebration activities I have implemented in my classes.

- On Halloween, I used our class meeting time to have a party. I encouraged my high school students to come dressed up, and I played spooky music as they entered the meeting. Through the creative use of Google Slides and breakout rooms, we spent the period playing Heads Up Seven Up. During the game, I unmuted mics, and the students had an opportunity to genuinely enjoy each other and the holiday. Students who never engaged with me unless prompted couldn't thank me enough for figuring out how to bring their childhood game to life for them one last time before they graduated.

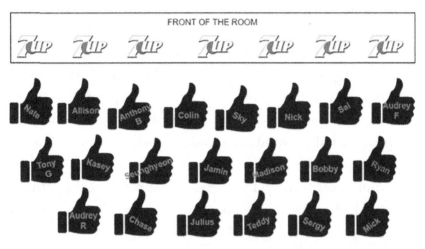

Image 3.1: An image from the online version of a class game of Heads Up Seven Up.

- On the last day of class, we held a winter break party in which we played a scavenger hunt. To play, I split up the teams into two and then held up an object. The students had to get the same item and return to their computer before the timer buzzed. Once the timer buzzed, I would say "reveal," and the students who had found it had to turn on their camera to reveal to me their object and earn a point for their team. The engagement was outstanding, and because we have a camera-choice policy in my district, it was the first time I had seen the majority of my students' faces.

OVERCOMING PUSHBACK

A virtual teaching environment, whether it's blended, hybrid, or full distance learning, requires you to assess your priorities. Pre-service teachers are repeatedly taught the importance of classroom management. If the classroom is not managed well, learning will be compromised. In a virtual setting, you won't have to worry about students passing notes or getting out of their seats at inappropriate times, but you will have to worry about a slew of different distractions. You know the type of chaos that's possible on a whole-class Zoom. You probably picture it in your sleep. In the online world of education, you may want to think of engagement as the new classroom management. Some teachers just want to get through their lessons and don't see the extreme value-add of engagement along the way. Here's how to address that viewpoint within yourself or others.

My job is to teach students, not entertain them. Some teachers struggle with the thought of using class time to engage students. They believe students should come to class motivated and ready to learn or that life can't always be entertaining, and school should prepare students for that reality. They resent the thought that the classroom teacher is somehow responsible for student participation. Those teachers are part of a century-old compliance model in which the school's infrastructure supported this belief and punished those who could not comply. Virtual learning, however, does not support this compliance model. Students aren't forced to sit in your classroom and deal with the ramifications of being off-task. Instead, the virtual learning model generates empowered learners who have a choice in whether or not they will pay attention or complete the tasks you have assigned. You no longer have the ability to send the student to the principal's office or assign detention if they don't demonstrate the behavior you seek. If you want learning to occur, you have to create an environment that motivates students to learn. You do that through intentional engagement. So, while in a face-to-face setting, you may say it's not your job to engage the students, but in a virtual learning setting, you won't be able to do your job without it.

I'm drowning in content, and I don't have the time or energy to worry about engagement. Beginning virtual teachers are in a constant existential crisis. Creating digital content in the form of learning artifacts is the primary focus of all new blended, hybrid, and digital learning teachers. Once they satisfy the threat of not having enough content, however, they realize they must focus on getting students to authentically engage in the content they created. It's not as difficult as it sounds. To avoid being overwhelmed, embed your engagement a little at a time. Start with one activity, gamified lesson, or celebration, and notice the difference in the energy of your class. As you get better at designing content, you will find pockets of time to focus your efforts on building engagement. The more you do it, the better you will become at it. When you see your students respond positively to your efforts and show an interest in the learning, you will be motivated to make more time for engagement.

THE HACK IN ACTION

John Meehan knows all about classroom engagement. He is a high school English teacher and instructional coach in Virginia and the author of the gamification book *EDrenaline Rush*. He's also co-founder of EMC2 Learning, a professional development site that teaches teachers how to be Engagement Engineers.

He says, "Content is still the number one passenger in the car 100 percent, but the driver is the human in front of you, and you want to design your lessons with the human in front of you in mind. We are teaching people, human beings, and we have to recognize that the human beings need to be seen as individuals and validated as those individuals before we attempt to just treat them as a bucket into which content can be dropped."

Meehan believes that engaging, well-designed lessons begin and end with understanding the needs of students, whether the class is face-to-face or virtual. He says educators know that practical-world relevance is critical for learning, but often, they don't know how to make the content relevant to their students. He gives the example of being taught how to solve math equations because "you may one day redesign your bedroom and need to know how much material to purchase." That misses the mark with students, as most have no experience designing a room or measuring material. Instead, he advises finding something relevant to their pop culture.

For example, instead of discussing the classic problem with the train going forty miles an hour toward a broken bridge and estimating how much time they will need to pull the brake, throw in some pop-culture zombies. Make the class a zombie apocalypse survival game in which two teams must now solve problems based on a horde of zombies chasing them.

"It's still solving math problems, but you have a little bit of zombie that makes the kids say, 'Well, we've got to solve it because there are zombies.'"

Meehan believes that gamification does more than just motivate students to participate; it changes the class culture. "One of the things that gamification does well when it is done correctly is it creates the sense that we are all in on the joke together and we are all playing a part for the same team. Even though there is a competition, there is a friendly nature that we are all sitting around the table playing for the same purpose."

Through play, students begin to develop relationships with each other. The other students become more than just peers, which means your class becomes more than just a class. It becomes a space where the students want to be with other people.

I witnessed firsthand how gamification could improve motivation and develop relationships when I used one of John's game templates to turn a boring lesson into an engaging one. During the first week of virtual learning, I wanted to provide my students with a digital literacy course to teach them how to navigate all the programs and tools used in the course. While the lesson would prove to be valuable to the students in time, on the surface, getting the students excited about learning digital literacy skills would be problematic. That is until I gamified the lesson utilizing The Floor Is Lava game template that John created and graciously offered for free through social media. Based on the popular children's game in which children try to cross a room without touching the ground because the floor is lava, I created a game for the class to compete against each other to finish the digital literacy tasks. See Image 3.2.

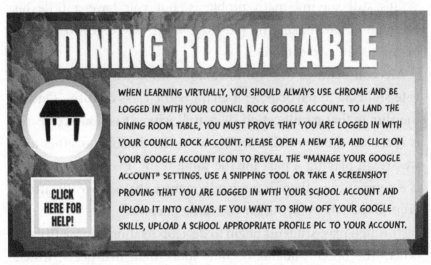

DINING ROOM TABLE

WHEN LEARNING VIRTUALLY, YOU SHOULD ALWAYS USE CHROME AND BE LOGGED IN WITH YOUR COUNCIL ROCK GOOGLE ACCOUNT. TO LAND THE DINING ROOM TABLE, YOU MUST PROVE THAT YOU ARE LOGGED IN WITH YOUR COUNCIL ROCK ACCOUNT. PLEASE OPEN A NEW TAB, AND CLICK ON YOUR GOOGLE ACCOUNT ICON TO REVEAL THE "MANAGE YOUR GOOGLE ACCOUNT" SETTINGS. USE A SNIPPING TOOL OR TAKE A SCREENSHOT PROVING THAT YOU ARE LOGGED IN WITH YOUR SCHOOL ACCOUNT AND UPLOAD IT INTO CANVAS. IF YOU WANT TO SHOW OFF YOUR GOOGLE SKILLS, UPLOAD A SCHOOL APPROPRIATE PROFILE PIC TO YOUR ACCOUNT.

CLICK HERE FOR HELP!

Image 3.2: This digital playing piece from The Class Is Lava activity
told students what to do to "land" the dining room table in the game.
In the process, students learned valuable digital literacy skills.

The moment I said we were playing a game, my students instantly became engaged, and as I explained the rules, the excitement continued to grow. I divided the class into four groups, gave them breakout rooms to work, and watched as they collaborated to complete each challenge and get all of their players to complete the tasks, cross the room, and try to be the first to exit the room.

When the activity was over, each team proudly announced their team's name—a task I didn't ask them to do. When I announced the winner, there was cheering and booing ... and none of this was because they were so excited about the digital literacy skills they had just acquired. For thirty minutes, they suspended belief, forgot they were in English class, and worked together to cross a room as quickly as possible while carefully making sure none of their classmates fell into lava.

John credits the success of the lesson to consent. He explains that the nature of play enhances learning and connection because it can't occur without consent. He says that students adopt the attitude of: "We don't have to play; we have consented to play."

What I learned during that lesson is that when my students collectively *consented* to play, they also *consented* to learn. With John's help, I purposefully embedded engagement into an assignment that helped build enthusiasm and community while teaching them something they previously had little to no desire to learn.

Teaching virtually does not have to be a struggle between complete alienation or chaos. While the innate nature of a virtual class takes away from how we have traditionally developed authentic relationships with our students, we can overcome this through intentional lesson design. When we embed engagement, we also embed learning. Once you accept that student engagement does not happen naturally in a virtual setting, you can build it into your curriculum through activities, gamified lessons, and celebrations. This builds enthusiasm for your course and its content one lesson at a time.

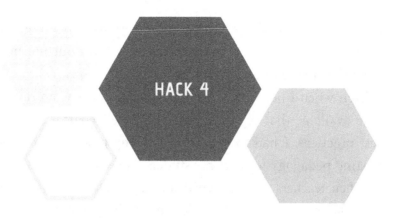

PLOT YOUR PEDAGOGY
Navigate the Gradual Release
of Responsibility

*The greatest sign of success for a teacher ... is to be able to
say, "The children are now working as if I did not exist."*
—MARIA MONTESSORI

THE PROBLEM: Teachers need a whole new way to teach in a virtual setting.

WHEN I WAS working toward my teacher certification, I took a course called Teacher Pedagogy. This class went over several models of instruction that were intended to aid me in my efforts to achieve my student learning goals. Not once did my professor discuss virtual pedagogy. Okay, to be fair, we hadn't explored this type of pedagogy because it didn't exist in the nineties when I was getting my undergraduate degree.

When I began studying edtech more seriously in my graduate program, the classes emphasized the new tools but not how to achieve learning in a digital format.

Even when I began my virtual teaching journey, no resources were available that supported a specific pedagogical strategy or best practices. I had to experiment in my practice and modify existing pedagogy to meet my students' needs.

When teachers were dropped into a remote learning environment due to COVID-19, I noticed to my disappointment that the conversation hadn't evolved much from my graduate work. Most of the discussions were based on what tools everyone was using and how to use them. Unfortunately, tools alone do not ensure learning.

THE HACK: Plot your pedagogy

To accomplish the "how" of virtual learning, we need to shift our thoughts regarding the act of teaching from being a process that is primarily reactive to one that is primarily proactive. Let's begin thinking of ourselves as navigators who have been charged with the task of creating a learning journey. To do this successfully, we need a map as we plot our new virtual pedagogy.

Because the overall goal of my virtual program was to cultivate student independence, I found Pearson and Gallagher's Gradual Release of Responsibility Model to be the most suitable "map" for a virtual setting. Their "I Do, We Do, You Do" format created a simplistic but strong and incredibly versatile foundation for my virtual teaching pedagogy.

I modified the Gradual Release of Responsibility model into a simple, five-step hack that plots student learning and assists teachers in their learning, regardless of the grade or curriculum. Many teachers have discovered this five-step version of the "I Do,

We Do, You Do" format to be a highly effective and flexible way to teach any class in an online setting.

Here's an overview of the five-step process:

1. **Identify Learning Objectives:** Where are we, and where are we going? Whether we're teaching students content or a skill, we need a measurable goal that identifies what we want the students to learn and how we will measure to determine their mastery.

2. **I Do:** This is the teacher-centered portion of the journey in which the teacher introduces the new content or models the skill for the students.

3. **We Do:** This is a collaboration phase between the teacher and the students. During this leg of the learning journey, the students practice their understanding of the content or skill while the teacher provides them with feedback and redirection.

4. **You Do:** This is the student-centered portion in which the student demonstrates what they have learned in a nonpunitive way without the teacher's assistance. This step determines if the student is ready to travel alone to the Demonstration of Mastery plot point or if they need to revisit the We Do phase for more assistance.

5. **Demonstration of Mastery:** A student demonstrates mastery when they independently complete a successful summative assessment.

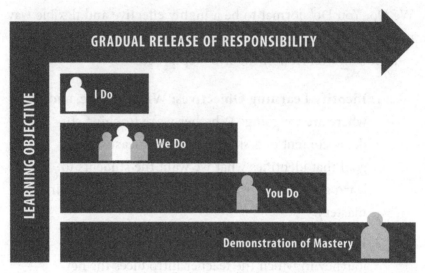

Image 4.1: The Gradual Release of Responsibility model.

Plot your pedagogy using these five steps, and you will create a successful teaching and learning structure so your students can master (and you can measure) their new content and skills.

WHAT **YOU** CAN DO TOMORROW

Here are a handful of steps you can take tomorrow to prepare yourself to be open to new ways of teaching online.

- **Remember your ultimate goal: to promote student learning.** No one wants to change just for change's sake. Make sure that any time you are changing the way you teach, it's for the ultimate benefit of those you serve. Hopefully, it makes your life easier at the same time. The GRR model does both.

- **Compare a current lesson to the Gradual Release of Responsibility (GRR) model**. You may discover that you are already using part of this process, even if parts of the lesson were labeled differently. Quickly dissect a typical current lesson to see if or how it lines up with this model. Do you see a Learning Objective, I Do, We Do, You Do, and a Demonstration of Mastery? Think about what parts of your current lesson hold high value (both to you and your students) and what parts bog everyone down and aren't worth the time you spend on them. If you are missing a step or two or they are in a different order, start looking at how you can redesign them in basic ways.

- **Browse for GRR sample lessons in your curricular area**. Search online for "Gradual Release of Responsibility" and your subject area, and scan through sample lessons. You may want to set a thirty-minute timer so you don't fall down a deep rabbit hole. You want to find inspiration and ideas at this point and see that plenty of help and resources exist when you are ready to give this model a try.

- **Get inspired to have an open mind and a growth mindset**. Remember that growth only happens outside of your comfort zone. Read or listen to your favorite authors or podcasters who inspire you to have an open mind and a growth mindset to prepare yourself for striving forward and benefitting you and your students.

A BLUEPRINT FOR FULL IMPLEMENTATION

This Blueprint section takes you through the Gradual Release of Responsibility model, showing two example lessons. The first example has the Learning Objective: "Students will be able to identify the layers of the atmosphere with 85 percent mastery." The second example has the Learning Objective: "Students will be able to identify the parts of a body paragraph and compose a body paragraph to include all the parts."

As you read the two examples, apply the information to your class, grade level, subject, and Learning Objectives. This is the section of the book you will likely revisit the most as you redesign your lessons to make teaching and learning more efficient, engaging, and successful for everyone.

STEP 1: Identify the Learning Objective.

As with all learning, the first step begins with identifying what students will learn. Since teaching virtually, I have an even stronger appreciation for my Learning Objectives. Because everything must be planned up front when you plot your lesson, it is important to clearly understand your end goal. Then choose your instructional strategies and tools based on that goal.

- Begin by identifying the content or skill you would like students to master.

- Next, determine if you will be creating a class or student goal. If you choose a class goal, the class will move through the plot points together, and their movement depends on the success of the class. However, if you choose a student goal, the students will move independently through the plot points, and each student's movement depends on the individual student's success.

- Then determine how you will measure mastery. For example, it is not enough to say, "Students will be able to identify the layers of the atmosphere." We have to determine a measurement to assess success. So, the Learning Objective could be, "Students will be able to identify the layers of the atmosphere with 85 percent mastery." By providing a specific percentage, we can assess when students achieve the objective. This is critical because it allows teachers to determine if they need to continue teaching the material or if students have achieved the desired outcome.

STEP 2: I Do.

This is the teacher-centered portion of the lesson. In face-to-face teaching, this typically means the teacher introduces the content or skill to the students through a lecture or modeling. However, in a virtual setting, teachers must adapt their instructional strategy to meet new needs associated with a change in setting. Digital instructional strategy options include:

- Teacher-generated screencasts
- Synchronous teacher-centered meetings
- Digital textbooks
- Preexisting videos
- eResources like digital articles and books
- Content-specific learning platforms

STEP 3: **We Do**.

In this section, teachers and students collaborate to develop an understanding of the new material. The teacher interacts with the students and confirms that they are using the new information or skill appropriately, or they offer redirection to help the student understand the new material. Multiple instructional strategies exist for teachers in a face-to-face setting to provide students with an opportunity to develop this learning. Examples include teacher-led discussions, worksheet completion, problem-solving, conferencing, read-alouds, and guided practice.

Because the We Do portion is collaborative, it can be challenging for the virtual teacher to provide this key step. However, digital collaboration tools make it easier for teachers and students to work together online. These tools include:

- Virtual discussions
- Slow chats
- Collaborative projects
- Collaborative eLearning platforms
- Interactive worksheets and documents

- Interactive videos

STEP 4: You Do.

Here, students practice working independently. The teacher-created lessons allow the students to complete the work independently and demonstrate their mastery of the material. This is the teacher's chance to determine if each student understands the material or needs additional instruction. In a face-to-face setting, students can demonstrate mastery through worksheets, writing prompts, equations, conferencing, oral responses, and presentations. In a virtual setting, "You Do" instructional strategies include:

- Digital quizzes and surveys

- Digital written prompts

- Video responses

- Use of formative assessment eLearning platforms

> **In a virtual setting, students are accountable for their learning, so it makes sense to offer a pedagogy format that gradually transfers the learning responsibility to them.**

If the Learning Objective stated that the student or class was to demonstrate 85 percent mastery, then the teacher will use the data from this formative and nonpunitive assessment to determine if the student or class is ready to be summatively assessed. If they score 85 percent or higher, they are ready to move on to the next plot point. If they do not, the student or class will return to the We Do plot point and work with the teacher to strengthen their mastery.

STEP 5: Demonstration of Mastery.

In this final step, now that all of the instructional heavy lifting is complete and the student has achieved the Learning Objective, you can move on to Demonstration of Mastery. This step is to summatively assess your students' learning. In other words, to confirm they know what you think they know. This may be the easiest part for you and your students. If you have appropriately selected your digital instructional strategies and used the information you obtained from the We Do and You Do portions of your lesson to assess instructional needs, then you can confidently move to this final step, knowing that your students are ready to prove themselves. For this section, create an assessment of their mastery of the Learning Objective. In a face-to-face setting, teachers do this via tests, essays, and projects. In a digital setting, options include:

- Projects
- Screencasts
- Conferences
- Digital tests
- Written responses

OVERCOMING PUSHBACK

For many teachers, teaching is an art, and learning is a result of their craft. After years in an in-person classroom, they naturally know how to meet their students' needs without having to overthink or critically plan. Like a country road they've driven a hundred times, they don't have to think about the next turn to get to their destination. They just make the turn and get there. They choose their activities based on what they know will work. They know what works because they have seen it work over and over in their classroom. However, nothing is natural about online teaching and learning. Prior to 2020, it was largely uncharted territory. As you know, to venture it alone without a map will result in frustration and a feeling of failure. Perhaps you or teachers you know have shared the following pushback and will benefit from the responses.

Teaching is an art, and I don't like to be confined to a structured pedagogy. The structure of Gradual Release of Responsibility is what makes it so conducive to a virtual environment. Considering that you will rarely be in the same space or time with your students, it is beneficial to have a format that you and your students can rely on for learning. In addition, in a virtual setting, students are accountable for their learning, so it makes sense to offer a pedagogy format that gradually transfers the learning responsibility to them.

But my kids aren't responsible, and a pedagogy that requires responsibility will fail them. This is a valid concern, especially for younger students. However, "gradual" is the beauty of the gradual release model. When done properly, the students will never really work alone until they have proven that they can complete the task independently. It's important to note that the plot points are fluid. A student can return to the We Do if they do not prove their independence in the You Do. Because the You Do is nonpunitive and solely exists for formative assessment purposes, think of it as a practice test. It is allowing the student to be independent in their learning without any negative ramifications. If they prove they are not ready to be independent, simply return to the We Do and try again until they master the material. They can't fail if you prevent them from entering the Demonstration of Mastery plot until they have proven they are capable of success.

THE HACK IN ACTION

Plotting the points of the Gradual Release of Responsibility has been the key to my virtual teaching success. I like that it provides a framework and helps me determine when learning has occurred. For example, I teach a high school writing class, and I've struggled to figure out when students have learned what I am teaching and when they are ready to submit their writing. In the past, I would teach a concept and then naively think the students had learned it just because I taught it. Unfortunately, I would later find that half the class still didn't have a clue. That changed when I started plotting my students' progress through the Gradual Release of Responsibility. Now I can gradually release the learning while assessing student learning, which means there are no more surprises. See Image 4.2 for my high school writing class lesson using the GRR model.

Sample Gradual Release of Responsibility model for a high school writing class

Learning Objective:	Students will be able to identify the parts of a body paragraph and compose a body paragraph to include all the parts.
I Do:	Using a teacher-centered lecture, I model how to write a body paragraph. Using a graphic organizer, I show them the parts of the body paragraph and then do a think-aloud as I write a sample.
We Do:	Using an interactive tool, the students practice writing the body paragraph while I watch and provide feedback. I ask the students to first identify the parts of a body paragraph and correct them in real time, providing additional instruction. The students then begin writing their own, and I continue to provide feedback and additional instruction as needed. I stay in this plot point as long as it takes for all students to properly identify the parts and appropriately write the paragraph.
You Do:	Students take a nonpunitive assessment to identify the parts of a body paragraph. Depending on the results, I will determine if the class is ready to move on to the plot point of Demonstration of Mastery or if they need to return to the We Do and receive additional support. If they do go back to the We Do, they will take the assessment again until they receive mastery.
Demonstration of Mastery:	Students independently write a body paragraph to summatively assess their learning. Because I have done the heavy lifting of providing the We Do for as long and as many times as they need it, my students can demonstrate their learning when they get to the Demonstration of Mastery.

Image 4.2: A sample lesson for a high school writing class.

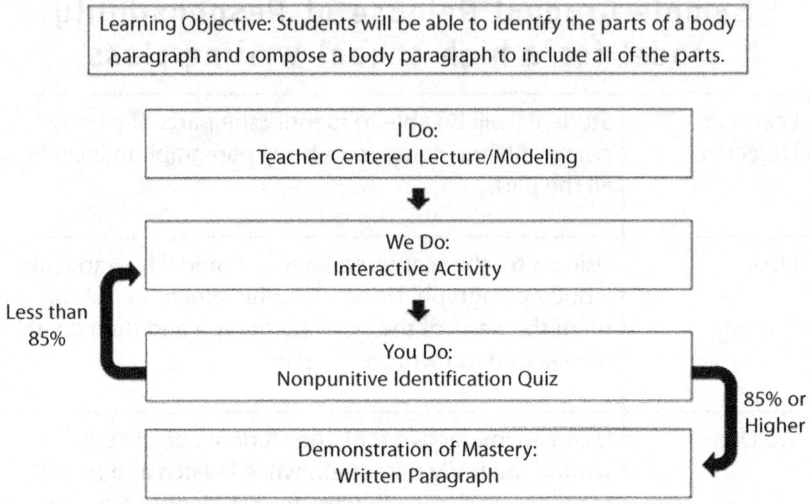

Learning Objective: Students will be able to identify the parts of a body paragraph and compose a body paragraph to include all of the parts.

I Do:
Teacher Centered Lecture/Modeling

We Do:
Interactive Activity

Less than 85%

You Do:
Nonpunitive Identification Quiz

85% or Higher

Demonstration of Mastery:
Written Paragraph

Image 4.3: The You Do phase determines if a student moves up to demonstrate mastery or repeats the We Do phase to continue the learning.

Because I teach high school, it is easy to understand how students can work through the plot points of the Gradual Release of Responsibility and achieve mastery. This can be more challenging for teachers of younger students.

Dr. Jessica Redcay, an award-winning elementary school teacher, explains how to use the model with elementary students. Redcay, the author of *VR Acclimation Model, STEMoscopte Model,* and *Ludus Learning,* says she likes using the gradual release model because it helps her empower students to move from Point A to Point B.

"I can't just assume that every student in my class will reach Point B if I tell or show the students. Rather, I intentionally use the gradual release model to ensure that every student receives the supports or scaffolds needed to stretch their learning a little bit further than what they already know."

When planning a GRR lesson, Dr. Redcay likes to compare it to when she learned how to drive.

"I had two parents with two different teaching approaches. One parent thought that I should automatically already know what to do because I saw people drive my entire life, and this parent also provided me with a quick, brief overview of what to do. I remember sitting in the driver's seat with a sense of loss because I knew that I wanted to drive, but I was confused about what I needed to learn or do."

By going from the I Do directly to the Demonstration of Mastery plot point, Dr. Redcay's parent unintentionally sabotaged her learning. Fortunately, she had another parent who innately understood the learning power of gradually releasing responsibility by breaking the skill of driving into smaller chunks.

"They would first demonstrate and explain a skill needed to drive ... then we practiced together, taking turns in the driver's seat going through the process. When I was in the driver's seat, they kept talking to me and telling me what to do. Eventually, they stopped telling me what to do, and although they were still in the car, I was driving on my own."

She demonstrated the mastery of her learning when she passed her driver's test, but she credits her success to her parent's ability to break a large concept into smaller chunks and guide her through the learning process. That lesson stuck with her, and today, when she plans a lesson, she models what she learned from driving and guides her students through the plot points of the Gradual Release of Responsibility.

Dr. Redcay is an advocate for the Gradual Release of Responsibility. In 2017, she presented at the Virginia Educational

Research Association Conference and shared research regarding students' vocabulary performances using the gradual release model.

"My research indicated that second grade students who learned through the gradual release model demonstrated significantly higher vocabulary scores than the control group. Simply put, second grade students gained more content-specific vocabulary words when a gradual release model was used in the classroom."

When she shifted to virtual learning in 2020, she naturally selected this model as a pedagogy to use for her students. She advises planning a lesson by chunking or breaking the content into smaller pieces that support the Learning Objective. She likes to use the tool **Nearpod** because it provides multiple instructional strategies to deliver each plot point.

"Nearpod was the tool that I used to create self-guided lessons using the gradual release model. I would show a demonstration video of a concept in a video clip (I Do). Then I would use the audio recorder to guide the students as they practiced the concept (We Do). Then I would provide the students with a slide where they can respond and try the concept on their own (You Do). Finally, students would respond with a video that I embedded using Flipgrid within Nearpod so they could demonstrate their mastery."

Like me, Dr. Redcay was never taught how to use the Gradual Release of Responsibility in a virtual setting, so both of us had to chart our own courses. She says she has found the model to be an effective way to plot student achievement and ultimately ensure their success.

In-person and virtual settings are wildly different and require unique teaching approaches in order to be effective. When you embrace the Gradual Release of Responsibility model and tweak it with virtual instructional strategies, you serve as a navigator who's taking your students on a learning journey through content and skill development. While it may feel uncomfortable to use a structured plan, in time, teachers will learn to depend on the predictability of the plot points and the service they provide for assessing student learning. While it may seem difficult to imagine elementary students being responsible for their learning, you will find that it is an equitable process that provides teachers the information they need to assess student learning and determine when their students have achieved the Learning Objective.

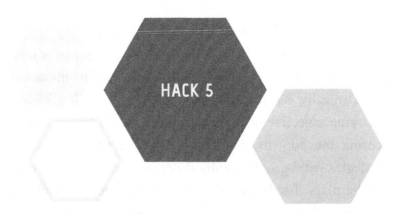

STRATEGIZE INSTRUCTIONAL STRATEGIES
Choose Strategies Before Tools

Tactics without strategy is the noise before defeat.
—SUN TZU

THE PROBLEM: With so many tools, you don't know which ones to pick

IMAGINE A PROFESSIONAL football team being told at the start of their season that all of their games would no longer be played on a turf field. Instead, they would have to play in six feet of water.

In theory, changing the setting of education from face-to-face to virtual learning should not have that big of an impact. Most would argue that it shouldn't be that difficult for professionals to adjust. We've all heard the advice to simply do what we do in the face-to-face classroom but do it on computers. However, if you view the change through the lens of an NFL player trying to adapt to playing in water, you will begin to see its impact.

Technically, it's still football, and they are still athletes with the same objective of getting the ball across the end zone and scoring touchdowns. But because they're in water now, their strategies will be significantly different. They can no longer rely on the plays that helped them win when they were playing on turf. This change in the playing field would impact their entire approach to the game.

The same holds true in the field of education. Whether you're teaching students together in person or in thirty different homes in front of thirty different computers, your goal of having students master the Learning Objective stays the same, but the way you accomplish that goal will have to change. Many of your previous strategies and techniques no longer work in the virtual setting.

Before choosing tech tools, choose your overarching instructional strategies—the techniques you use to help students become independent strategic learners and thinkers.

The Gradual Release of Responsibility gives you a game plan to follow, but you still need to know which instructional strategies work best for you and your students at the different plot points of the pedagogy. You may find this surprising, but the virtual setting lends itself to more instructional strategies than a face-to-face setting, which is why transitioning from face-to-face to virtual learning can be so overwhelming. With each new instructional strategy you adopt, you need to rely on an edtech tool to help you execute it. Many teachers become overburdened by the number of tools on the market, and in a race to learn them all, they have yet to master one.

THE HACK: Strategize instructional strategies

Before choosing tech tools, choose your overarching instructional strategies—the techniques you use to help students become independent strategic learners and thinkers. The goal is to deliver your instruction in a way that makes sense for you and your students. You'll want to base your strategies on your teaching style, your educational philosophies, and your comfort level. There are no one-size-fits-all instructional strategies. As in a face-to-face classroom, you get to decide which strategies you feel most comfortable using.

In the Gradual Release of Responsibility model, instruction occurs at the I Do and We Do plot points. In the I Do, your instruction is teacher-centered, and you'll want to choose instructional strategies that allow you to deliver the content or skill to your students. At the We Do plot point, you collaborate with students and provide instruction and feedback, so you want to choose strategies that offer an interactive component. See examples of instructional strategies in the A Blueprint for Full Implementation section of this chapter.

Once you have chosen your instructional strategies, it's time to choose your essential tools. Instead of learning every tool out there, focus on the ones that support your learning strategies. Tools should make it easy for you to learn, teach, and engage your students. Edtech tools run rampant online, so you'll want to invest your time and energy in learning the best tools that support your instruction.

The next section helps you narrow down the options.

WHAT **YOU** CAN DO TOMORROW

- **Research options for virtual learning instructional strategies for your subject and grade level.** Choose a few new ones to build up your instructional strategy arsenal.

- **Identify the tools you currently master.** Analyze why you use them and determine if they support your instructional strategies in the I Do or We Do plot of the Gradual Release of Responsibility. Choose a new tool or two, ask your PLN for their experience with the tools, and watch the tutorials to confirm you're comfortable with the choices.

- **Ask your district technology coaches and librarians for resources.** They may offer ideas for instructional strategies and access to tools that support learning in the Gradual Release of Responsibility. Consider their suggestions and choose tools that fit your style.

- **Ask colleagues and your PLN about their favorite strategies and tools.** See if you can observe them teaching the strategy or tool in action. This is a great way to learn how to use new strategies and tools and see if they will support your chosen instructional strategies. Be brave and ask another teacher to share what they are doing and offer to invite them to your class in return.

A BLUEPRINT FOR FULL IMPLEMENTATION

STEP 1: Identify instructional strategies for I Do.

The objective of the I Do plot of the Gradual Release of Responsibility is to introduce a new skill or content to the class for the first time. For face-to-face delivery of content, teachers have traditionally used the instructional strategy of teacher-centered lecture; for building skills, they may have used teacher modeling. Both of these strategies are still effective in a digital setting. However, in an asynchronous setting, the teacher would have to pre-record a video of the lecture. Teachers can deliver I Do instruction via strategies such as:

- Recorded teacher-centered lecture
- Recorded teacher modeling
- Content-specific learning platforms
- Digital textbooks
- eResources like videos, podcasts, websites, articles, eJournals, and eBooks

STEP 2: Identify instructional strategies for We Do.

The objective of the We Do plot of the Gradual Release of Responsibility is to create opportunities to interact with the students while they begin practicing what they have learned. The teacher provides real-time feedback to support student learning and encourages exploration of the topic. Many strategies teachers use in a face-to-face setting can be adjusted for use in a virtual setting. Teachers can deliver We Do instruction via such strategies as:

- Student-centered class discussions
- Teacher-led guided practice
- Problem-solving with real-time checks for understanding
- Interactive worksheets and documents
- Presentations
- Discussions
- Slow chats

STEP 3: Choose your essential tools.

Thousands of edtech tools flood the market; however, not all tools will support your instructional strategies. I have heard countless stories of frustrated teachers forced to sit through professional development to learn a new tool that they didn't think would fit into their curriculum or teaching style. This is why I advocate for identifying your strategies first and then finding the tools that fit them. Adopting a new digital tool into your curriculum is a big investment in time and energy that you don't want to squander on the newest, shiniest tool on the internet. Be strategic with the tools you trust for you and your students. Make sure they match your desired instructional strategy, meet the learning needs of your students, are dynamic enough to be used repeatedly, and fit within your or your district's budget.

Instructional strategies tend to be personal because how we choose to deliver our content is the artistry of our craft. It makes sense that selecting tools to support our craft is also a personal process. With so many tools on the market, I have seen teachers pressured into investing time learning a product that doesn't support their teaching style or the needs of their students simply because it's a cool tool. In addition, I've seen teachers unnecessarily invest time and money into trying to master all the tools out there because they somehow associate more tools with being better teachers.

To normalize the practice of having no shame in your tech-tool game, I will share *all* the tools I use to instruct students in my synchronous and asynchronous virtual course. They are:

1. Canvas (my Learning Management System)

2. Google Slides

3. Screencastify

4. Actively Learn

That's it. Note that although I use four tools, I am not limited to only four instructional strategies. I've strategically chosen these tools to deliver my complex content because they are dynamic and fit perfectly with my teaching style and curriculum. Here are more details about how I use each of these four tools:

Canvas: My district-selected Learning Management System, Canvas, is essential for housing all of my learning artifacts and assessments. However, it also provides instructional strategies. For the I Do plot point, I can use Canvas to record and post asynchronous teacher-centered video lectures or audio recordings that deliver content to my students. For the We Do plot point, I use Canvas's discussion board for student-centered slow chats, conferencing, and teacher-led class discussions.

Google Slides: This dynamic tool is free, and it's an important one in my teaching arsenal because it makes my instruction and student learning visible. For the I Do plot point, Slides has replaced my chalkboard, and I use it to provide the visual content to support my asynchronous teacher-centered video lectures and synchronous teacher-centered lectures. Because Slides can be interactive, it is an incredibly powerful tool during the We Do plot point in the form of an interactive worksheet. It allows me to see student learning in real time. I simply assign each student a slide and set my view to grid view, and I can see all the students as they complete their work. I can provide feedback to support student learning.

When I used Slides during a synchronous lesson, my Learning Objective was to teach the students how to develop a thesis statement. For the I Do, I use the instructional strategy of teacher-centered lecture to model how to dissect a prompt to create a thesis statement. I share my screen with the class and model the work on the first slide, similar to how one would use a chalkboard in a face-to-face setting. After providing that instruction, I stop sharing my screen and transition to the We Do plot. Each student is assigned a slide as an interactive whiteboard.

I set my view to grid view and can see each student trying to put into practice what they have learned. Because I can see each slide in real time, I can provide critical feedback to the student to support their learning. I add purple stars to communicate mastery to the student. In addition, students have access to their peers' work, which provides them with peer modeling. I have found it an incredibly valuable instructional strategy during the We Do plot, as some students learn effectively by watching how their classmates do it.

Screencastify: This is a free Chrome screencasting extension to record your teacher-centered instruction. When I use it with Google Slides, I can create multisensory teacher-centered instruction for the I Do plot point that my students can access as often as needed.

Actively Learn: This powerful online curriculum platform supports English, Science, and Social Studies. It is a subscription service that does offer a free version; however, the paid service provides the most instructional strategies. Actively Learn is like the Swiss Army knife of virtual instruction and solves our We Do plot point problems. For example:

- Actively Learn can turn all of your content into an interactive activity to support student learning.

- It makes my novels, poems, short stories, work-sheets, presentations, and videos interactive, as the service allows me to embed questions directly into the sources.

- For synchronous interaction, we can assess student learning by embedding short-answer questions that create an opportunity for dialogue between the student and teacher. A student can read or view a section, while the teacher checks for understanding by embedding a question. (For more about how to create a culture of inquiry as you teach, read *Hacking Questions* by Connie Hamilton.)

- Once the student answers, the teacher replies, similar to an online chat, and provides the feedback students need in real time to support their learning.

- If the class is asynchronous, we can provide a multiple-choice question and preloaded feedback for the student, explaining why their choice was correct or incorrect. Whether we are teaching content or skill, Actively Learn's interactive features validate student learning and provide the necessary feedback to deepen their understanding before moving on to the You Do plot of the Gradual Release of Responsibility.

OVERCOMING PUSHBACK

Let's all acknowledge that virtual teaching causes a tremendous amount of self-doubt because what has always worked for us in the face-to-face classroom not only doesn't work, but it also may not even be an option anymore. As a result, teachers naturally seek comfort in finding a tool to bridge the gap between what they used to do and what they now must do. This results in tool overload (using too many tools) or tool paralysis (not being able to decide which tools to use). The goal is to find a balance by using tools that serve your pedagogy and instructional strategy. You may think or hear the following pushback.

Doesn't a greater variety of tools mean better teaching? While it certainly does not hurt to be well-versed in what tools are available and how they could support your instruction, the reality is that investing time in learning a tool that does not support your curriculum, style, or student needs is a waste of time. In addition, with every new tool you adopt in your class, you will need to spend valuable class time teaching your students how to use it. It makes sense to limit your tools to the ones that truly speak to you, your students, and your curriculum, and use them in various ways.

I have no idea which tools to select. The beauty of adopting the Gradual Release of Responsibility as your primary pedagogy for developing mastery of content and skill is that it creates a foundation for you to begin making your instructional decisions. The specific plot points call for different strategies. You determine which strategies you feel comfortable implementing at each plot point. Once you begin identifying the approaches, you investigate which tools will support your plan. For example, if you choose teacher-centered videos as an instructional strategy, you can begin to select a tool by searching for a screencasting tool to support your instructional strategy. Unfortunately, many teachers work backward by selecting the technology without any real strategy on how it will support their pedagogical decisions. This type of planning is problematic, as without a strong pedagogical foundation, you are simply relying on a tool to be fully responsible for student learning. To find the best tools for you and your classes, do a bit of research, check with your edtech leaders and librarians, and ask other teachers and your PLN for their ideas.

THE HACK IN ACTION

As a high school teacher, I am lucky to have only one curriculum to teach, and I get to teach it to students who have mastered independent learning skills. However, my elementary colleagues have multiple curriculums, and their younger students need more support. This means that elementary teachers will naturally have more instructional strategies to use and more tools to support their use.

An award-winning elementary teacher and technology

facilitator, Christina Ortega, is responsible for teaching reading, writing, and math to students with underdeveloped independent learning skills. Ortega says she believes educators "think that there needs to be a one-to-one correspondence between instructional strategies." She advises her staff to "use one to three tools that work best for you and your learners as your 'go-to' tools and gradually add if necessary." She argues that effective educators use fewer tools but use them in versatile ways for various strategies.

Ortega shares the following list of her favorite instructional strategies and tools and how she uses them in her classes:

- **Padlet** offers a space for reciprocal teaching and Socratic seminar and can also be used as an informal assessment tool. It works well for the I Do and We Do areas of Ortega's vocabulary instruction. Padlet is a versatile tool and includes a video function to record student responses for informal assessment, headings to organize discussions for Socratic seminar and reciprocal teaching, and an image search tool to support visualization for vocabulary development.

- **Nearpod** is a titan hub in its versatility, as it also provides I Do and We Do instructional strategies for language development. As a tool for a student-paced lesson, it supports the I Do plot point; it can also be used in the We Do plot, as teachers can embed questions and create interactive videos that support student learning.

- **Seesaw** has a drawing tool and a microphone that allow teachers to provide We Do instructional strategies. Ortega uses it to teach spelling and writing. She follows the science of reading and provides direct instruction via scripted programs to model and use guided practice. Seesaw allows students to demonstrate their learning and the teacher to provide timely feedback.

- For math classes in the I Do stage, Ortega uses **Google Slides, Edpuzzle** for interactive videos, and **Seesaw** for task analysis. For the We Do plot in math, she uses **Seesaw** for self-assessment and **Zoom's** breakout rooms for student-centered academic discussions.

Teachers were thrown into the deep end of the education pool when classrooms switched from face-to-face to virtual learning. Like an NFL team forced to finish their season in a pool, teachers had to make major adjustments on short notice, especially in their instructional strategies. Now that most teachers have gained some experience with virtual teaching (or blended, flex, remote, or online teaching), it's time to be more strategic about instructional strategies and tools, whether you teach elementary or secondary grades. Remember that effective virtual learning is not measured by how many tools you use. Instead, it is measured by how effectively you use the tools to engage your students in the learning and create the best learning outcomes.

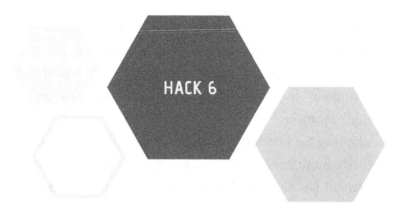

ASSESS YOUR ASSESSMENT
Take a Look at Your Teaching

Change the way you look at things, and
the things you look at change.
—WAYNE DYER

THE PROBLEM: It's hard to tell if students are learning in virtual classes

"OHHH!" EVERY TEACHER loves to hear students make this sound. It means students understand what we are explaining, they get it now, and learning has occurred. We can tell by the look on their face that they have developed comfort with the new material or skill, and we can move on.

Unfortunately, we don't get to hear that audible "Ohhh!" and see the accompanying facial expression during virtual learning. Because of the space-time continuum, we are rarely in the same space at the same time to experience our students' learning. If we

107

are teaching in a synchronous environment, the norm of muting the students' mics prevents us from hearing this acknowledgment. Teachers must be more intentional with understanding their students' learning and recognizing the digital version of an "Ohhh!" moment.

Adopting the Gradual Release of Responsibility means that we must rely more heavily on assessment. It's important to note that assessment has earned a bad reputation in terms of the pressure it puts on students and teachers. By assessing your assessment, you will reframe the way you and your students think about it and develop a healthier relationship with it. It will only be used to determine when the student should move on to the next plot point. Think of this movement as similar to a video game in which the player earns access to a new level by completing a boss battle using the newly acquired skill or knowledge of the game to defeat the bad guy. The We Do and You Do plot points require students to demonstrate learning before moving on to the fully independent plot point of Demonstration of Mastery, which gamers may refer to as The Ultimate Boss Battle. In virtual learning, teachers need to rely on assessment in ways they never had to in a face-to-face classroom.

In person, teachers can determine understanding by using instructional strategies that require very little prep or execution. Simply having a conversation with a class can provide teachers with a lot of information to drive instruction. Unfortunately, virtual learning does not afford the same ease of assessment. In virtual learning, determining understanding must be intentional, planned, and prepped. Unfamiliar with this new burden, many teachers find themselves frustrated by virtual learning assessments. The amount of time to plan and execute can be excessive, and the vulnerability of possible cheating can be discouraging. However, constantly measuring student learning is a critical component of successful virtual learning, as the information you receive from the assessments will determine if the student can move forward within the Gradual Release of Responsibility.

To be successful, teachers will benefit by spending a bit of time upfront to assess their assessments. It doesn't work to substitute in-person assessment practices into a virtual classroom. Instead, let's examine the what, how, and why of assessment as we redefine our classrooms.

THE HACK: Assess your assessment

I believe that quizzes and tests measure how I'm doing as the teacher … not how my students are doing. Instead of using assessments to rate my students' learning punitively, I use them nonpunitively to drive my instruction. I began adopting this philosophy when I developed my virtual course and realized that I wasn't confident in my virtual teaching skills. So, I started giving quizzes to see how I was doing. I used the data to determine if my new virtual instructional strategies were effective. Now I use quizzes (formative assessments) as a best practice to drive all of my instruction. The kind of assessment I use depends on which plot of the Gradual Release of Responsibility I am in.

For students to pass through the Gradual Release of Responsibility, they must demonstrate their learning in the We Do and You Do plot points. Formative assessments are the best way for teachers to determine where students are in their learning and what they need from the teacher to reach the Learning Objective. Assessments along the way should not be used as punitive grades because the students are still engaged in the process of learning.

Formative assessment must quickly and in real time determine learning; otherwise, students' movement through the Gradual Release of Responsibility will be stalled, and learning will stop.

The Demonstration of Mastery plot point is a summative assessment grand finale. This is when you measure student learning and report it as a grade. Given the independent nature of virtual learning, teachers must create evaluations that don't allow students to cheat. You can easily accomplish this by creating assignments that are in Level 4 of Webb's Depth of Knowledge. This means teachers ask students to use their learning to create something from nothing and ultimately make their learning visible. When students are asked to synthesize their learning and demonstrate it by creating something new, teachers can be confident that what they are seeing is a true reflection of student learning.

Before I used the Gradual Release of Responsibility model, I would lecture on topics and assume the students would need support. For example, when I taught *The Great Gatsby*, I spent time on the green light symbolism in the story, as it was important for understanding the text. Before using a formative assessment, I would spend two class periods discussing the symbol and providing evidence from the text to support student learning. It turns out that once I formatively assessed their initial understanding of the text before launching into my green light lecture, I found that the symbol was quite obvious to the students. They all understood what it meant, which meant I could bank the two class periods I had planned for the green light lecture and use it for other purposes to support student learning.

WHAT YOU CAN DO TOMORROW

- **Assess your existing assessments.** Consider your current assessments in light of the We Do and You Do phases, where you are still gradually releasing the responsibility of the learning to your students. Do the scores count toward their grade? Is it possible for students to cheat? Is it hard to see a clear connection between the assessment data and the Learning Objective? If your answer to any of these questions is yes, then you need to adjust your assessments or adopt new ones that make more sense for you and your students and use everyone's time wisely.

- **Discover digital assessment tools in your LMS.** If your LMS already includes assessment tools, these options can make the process efficient for you and your students. They won't have to leave the site, and you can easily access the feedback. In the We Do and You Do plots, it is essential to find tools that can provide real-time feedback. Choose a tool that does more than just grade; look for options to hold an interactive chat with students or provide immediate feedback on correct and incorrect information. The assessment tool should confirm areas of strengths and provide additional instruction where the student may need it.

- **Chat with colleagues about assessments.** Reach out to your PLN or curriculum or grade-level partners and talk about how everyone measures student learning and how they use it to drive their instructional practice. Make a note of the best ideas that might work well for you.

- **Read up on Webb's Depth of Knowledge (DOK).** Look online for examples of Depth of Knowledge Level 4 in your curricular area. It can be challenging to reimagine tests and create an assessment that makes student learning visible without the opportunity to cheat. DOK 4 can help.

A BLUEPRINT FOR FULL IMPLEMENTATION

STEP 1: Refresh your We Do assessments.

During the We Do plot point of the Gradual Release of Responsibility, teachers and students collaborate to help students develop their understanding of the new material or skill. This replaces the in-person classroom instruction where the teacher takes questions, identifies areas that need to be clarified, and pushes thinking, so it would be inappropriate for the work in this phase to impact students' grades. During this phase, the teacher provides an opportunity for students to experiment and practice the new learning so they can reach the Learning Objective. Then teachers determine student knowledge and provide feedback to help develop the learning.

Ideally, the nonpunitive assessments used during this plot will:

- Be interactive

- Provide real-time feedback (especially in a synchronous environment) so the students' learning continues to progress

- Create opportunities for the student and teacher to engage with each other to push learning forward

- Offer interventional feedback (such as a multiple-choice quiz that automatically grades and provides an explanation)

- Cause students to exclaim, "Ohhh! I get it now!"

See Image 6.1 for an example of how I use Actively Learn to post questions, see student answers, score their answers, and provide feedback in real time.

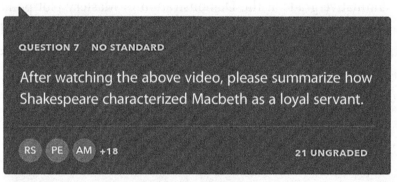

Image 6.1: This example shows a slice of We Do learning in action, as a student posts a response to the teacher's question so the teacher can provide feedback in real time.

STEP 2: Reimagine your You Do assessment.

During the You Do plot point of the Gradual Release of Responsibility, students are no longer receiving instruction, and they have to demonstrate mastery of the new skill or content independently. At this point, the assessment needs to be comprehensive with what it is measuring, but it also needs to provide feedback in real time. It does not have to be interactive because if the student does not demonstrate mastery, they will go back to the We Do plot point and receive additional instruction. It is simply to identify if the student is ready to prove their mastery for a summative grade at the Demonstration of Mastery plot point or if they need to return to the We Do plot point for additional support. If these descriptions don't sound like your assessments at this stage, it's time to reimagine your You Do assessment and how you are determining students' progress in learning.

Note that students may need to retake the assessment in the You Do stage multiple times before they have mastered the content or skill. Again, this assessment is not for a grade; it is only used as a tool to determine if the student needs more support or if they are ready to be summatively assessed.

See Image 6.2 for an example of how I used Actively Learn to generate automatically graded multiple-choice questions that provided instant data. I could determine which students were ready to move on to the Demonstration of Mastery finale and which students needed to return to the We Do phase to receive more instruction. This data dashboard also allowed me to see the exact areas to address with students.

Name	Time	Notes	Vocab	Translate	TTS	Q1 Q2 Q3 Q4 Q5 Q6 Q7 Q8 Q9 Q10 Q11 Q12 Q13
CLASS AVERAGE	43m	.	.	.	.	
Student names (blocked out)	48m	.	.	.	.	
	36m	.	.	.	.	
	34m	.	.	.	.	
	27m	.	.	.	.	
	39m	.	.	.	.	
	37m	.	.	.	.	
	17m	.	.	.	.	
	1h 5m	.	.	.	.	
	37m	.	.	.	.	
	43m	.	.	.	.	
	50m	.	.	.	.	
	47m	.	.	.	.	
	27m	.	.	.	.	
	1h 4m	.	.	.	.	
	16m	.	.	.	.	
	57m	.	.	.	.	
	1h 15m	.	.	.	.	
	39m	.	.	.	.	
	1h 28m	.	.	.	.	
	47m	.	.	.	.	

Image 6.2: This example shows a slice of You Do learning in action, as the teacher can see the accuracy and timing of student answers all at once to determine how best to help each student.

STEP 3: Choose the best assessment for the Demonstration of Mastery.

During the Demonstration of Mastery plot point, students officially prove their mastery of the content or skill. Quite simply, they are demonstrating their learning. This phase is a summative assessment and the results are graded, but at this point, the results should be positive since the teacher took measures in the We Do and You Do phases to filter areas of weakness and provide intervention to support each student's development of mastery. The biggest area of concern for Demonstration of Mastery is to create an evaluation that makes it impossible to cheat.

Students will recognize that the assessments in the We Do and You Do phases are designed to help them understand the content or skill and are for their benefit.

Because students will not be in the same space or possibly even the same time as the classroom teaching, cheating is often easy for students in a virtual setting. However, you can prevent it by going as low as possible with Webb's Depth of Knowledge. If you go to Depth of Knowledge 4, which requires students to synthesize information and transfer knowledge to solve a problem or create a new product, cheating is no longer a concern because students will literally be creating something new to demonstrate their learning. The goal here is to make their learning visible.

See Image 6.3 for an example of a Demonstration of Mastery assessment in action. I polled students to determine what they didn't like about the book they just completed. Then I asked them to reimagine it to create a new story. This assignment cannot be copied from anyone else, and it can't be completed without a mastery of the content.

Because you are curious of how Finny's narrative would impact the book, you will have the opportunity of solving the problem associated with point of view.

Therefore, you will re-imagine the text from Finny's point of view... instead of Gene's.

To begin, you will identify the 10 most significant scenes from the story and re-imagine them from Finny's point of view.

You will then use google slides and a work-around of Story Board That to help illustrate the new format of the book.

Use this slide-show graphic organizer to complete the project:

SLIDE SHOW

Image 6.3: This example shows the teacher's instructions to students in a Demonstration of Mastery assessment that fits the criteria of a best practice in virtual teaching summative assessments.

OVERCOMING PUSHBACK

It's challenging to go to a teacher conference, social media platform, or even a lounge without hearing the negative rhetoric around testing. Due to factors outside of our limited classroom control, testing has received a negative reputation and has become somewhat of a dirty word in education. However, to help serve our students, we have to reframe the word and see assessment as nothing more than gathering information. It doesn't have to be hurtful, shameful, or biased. It can simply just determine what we, as teachers, still need to do to fulfill our promise to teach our students. Consider these two common areas of pushback and the responses.

I want my time in class to be spent on instruction, not assessment. If assessment is done right, it can make your instructional time more efficient because you will use the information derived from it to drive your instruction. Your formative assessments will tell your students exactly what they need from you to understand the Learning Objective. Remember my story about *The Great Gatsby* in The Hack section of this chapter? When you use formative assessments to show you, as the teacher, what your students still need to learn, you can make the learning more productive and engaging for all involved.

Students are overwhelmed with testing demands, and I don't want to add to it. Note that I am making a clear distinction between formative and summative assessments. Formative assessment is low-stakes and nonpunitive and simply provides the teacher with the information they need to determine the next steps to support their students. Summative assessment serves as a ledger for the students' mastery of the Learning Objective. When done appropriately, students will recognize that the assessments in the We Do and You Do phases are designed to help them understand the content or skill and are for their benefit. The scores won't hurt their grade or get them in trouble at home. When you explain to the students that formative assessments are not used to judge but rather to help them, they quickly begin to engage in the process and collaborate in their learning.

They also become empowered by understanding how to use data to measure their learning and how to use tools to advocate for their education. In addition, they feel successful when they use the Gradual Release of Responsibility model to learn and achieve mastery at the summative assessment plot point. Students are often thrilled to see that their recorded grades will be high. It allows them to trust in you, your class, and their ability to stick with something to learn it to the mastery level. It's an incredibly valuable skill that will serve them well as adults.

THE HACK IN ACTION

It can be difficult to create assessments that measure mastery at the Level 4 Depth of Knowledge or even to understand what that means. Joe Welch, an award-winning middle school social studies teacher, shares his methods as he describes how he evaluates student learning in a masterful way.

Instead of relying on multiple-choice questions or Blue Book essay questions to analyze the Demonstration of Mastery, Welch goes to the Level 4 Depth of Knowledge and asks his students to create something from nothing to demonstrate their mastery.

He says, "I want the students to have some representation of their content knowledge or their research. I want them to have a physical end product that they created that allows them to share their perspective."

Welch believes that teachers can build creativity into the assessment and that "literacy will build creativity and creativity will build literacy." He wants students to be creative, to embrace their views, and to create something from nothing as the best way to make their learning visible. He admits that the sheer distance of students not being able to be in the same room makes evaluating them in this manner more difficult. To provide a space for kids to create while they are at a distance, Welch often uses these three tools as part of his summative assessments:

- **GarageBand** (an audio app for creating music or podcasts)

- **Clips** (an app for video editing)

- **Keynote** (a presentation app that works well for virtual learning students to create and demonstrate their learning)

As a social studies teacher, Welch measures student learning by creating stop-motion photography, soundtracks, and video documentaries. For example, when he teaches his students about Jamestown, his Learning Objective is for students to understand why the people of Jamestown struggled. After providing them with primary documents and working them through the I Do, We Do, and You Do plot points of the Gradual Release of Responsibility, he wants them to show him what they have learned in the Demonstration of Mastery plot.

He instructs his students: "Give me three reasons Jamestown struggled to survive, and instead of writing an essay, solve the problem by showing me and being creative with Legos or Play-Doh."

He then asks them to photograph their creations and use creative apps such as the ones listed earlier. They may create projects using anything from stop-motion animation to hip-hop tracks to documentaries. The creative results make their learning visible and allow Welch to assess their mastery of learning. He has found that students respond well to the Level 4 Depth of Knowledge because they do more than just memorize the material to get an A on the test. He says, "Did they learn the content? … yes. Did they memorize it? … no. Will they remember this? … YES!"

When learning is moved from the classroom to a virtual space, we can no longer rely on our natural teacher superpower to determine when student learning has occurred. Instead, we must assess our assessments to make sure we are intentional about measuring student learning and evaluating how we can support the students in their quest for mastery. When educators and students reframe their understanding of assessment, it will help students achieve the Learning Objectives and empower them with the tools of evaluation and advocacy that will serve them throughout school and as adult learners.

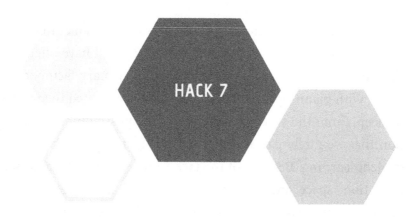

PERSONALIZE STUDENT LEARNING PATHS

Create Equity by Meeting Individual Needs

Two roads diverged in a wood and I—I took the one less traveled by, and that has made all the difference.

—ROBERT FROST

THE PROBLEM: It's hard to meet each student's individual needs in virtual learning

IN *BACK TO the Future*, Doc Brown repeatedly warns Marty to be cautious about his decisions in the past and future, as even the slightest disturbance can completely alter the space-time continuum. Think of virtual learning as a major disturbance that has altered the educational space-time continuum.

Throughout the existence of education, space and time have directly impacted in-person student learning and have often created unintended inequities, as they are the primary factors associated with planning. Space and time have ingratiated themselves so deeply into the way we think about the possibilities of education that we rarely pay any attention to their negative impact on student learning. Because of the face-to-face nature of traditional education, space and time have committed the biggest assault on student success. They have restricted the scope and sequence of learning, often resulting in punitive actions and restrictive learning opportunities.

In in-person classrooms, for example, the first grader who isn't able to get all of his work done during the forty-five-minute time slot must remain inside for recess to work with the teacher. The child misses valuable socialization and a much-needed brain break, resulting in negative feelings about learning simply because he needed more time than his peers to complete the work.

Another example is the high school student whose grades drop because she needs to work an after-school job. Her teachers assign homework to complete outside of the school day, but the student doesn't have time after school to complete the assigned work, and she falls asleep, exhausted, after getting off work late. She's punished with a bad grade and identified on the report card as a deficient learner.

The punitive nature of time can be more subtle. Think of the students who learn quickly and master the content faster than their peers. They squander their learning and, subsequently, enthusiasm for learning while waiting for their classmates and teacher to catch up.

Finally, the teacher who understands that student choice improves learning outcomes but cannot offer this model because the limited space of the classroom makes it difficult for the teacher to have thirty students completing thirty different assignments.

It's hard to fall in love with learning when you are given no choice, punished for not learning fast enough or having enough time to complete the work, or being told to hold on and wait for everyone else.

Online learning and all the possibilities it affords can alter the shape of education because teachers and students are no longer bound to the restrictions of space and time. Whether they are in a face-to-face classroom with a blended or hybrid class or fully remote with a virtual class, teachers generally don't have to worry about having students hit the same benchmarks of assessment at the same time because the learning is not restricted by the classroom boundaries or the bell. With the endless possibilities of the LMS, students can learn where time and space have minimal restrictions. However, teachers need help creating equity and meeting individual student needs in a virtual environment.

THE HACK: Personalize student learning paths

Online lessons with strong pedagogy and assessment help students experience their own learning adventures based on needs or choice, resulting in personalized learning. Teachers can proactively generate personalized learning pathways while eliminating the punitive and restrictive parts of traditional face-to-face instruction.

To put it simply, teachers can personalize student learning paths by giving students exactly what they need at the exact time they need it. By introducing diverse learning artifacts and assessment tools, teachers build content in their LMS that will allow students to move through their learning at an appropriate pace for their choice of learning.

When I developed my virtual course, I began learning new and effective instructional strategies that I wanted to use in my face-to-face class. It didn't take long before my adoption of those strategies created a productive blended learning environment. Around the third year of teaching in a blended model, after repeatedly reading about the inequity caused by relying on homework as an instructional strategy, I began to see the inequity for myself. The analytics showed whether learning occurred and how much time students spent on assignments. Despite having a leveled English classroom where all students in my class were assigned to my class because they had demonstrated similar literacy skills, their analytics showed they all had unique needs, which required some to need more time than others to complete assignments. I started to contemplate the concept of equity and how having the same expectations for students to complete activities was unfair. I got the ambitious idea to create a homework-free classroom.

For example, through the analytics, I observed a female student who needed the entire class period to read the short story and needed an additional hour that night to complete the reading assignment associated with the chapter. Sitting right next to her was a male student whose analytics showed he could complete all the work within thirty minutes of class time. His analytics showed he spent the last half of class sitting idle because he had completed his work. That discrepancy didn't feel right. It was wrong to make one student work the entire period and then have to work an additional hour later that evening simply because I needed everyone to be in the same place when they walked into the room the next day. In addition, I felt it was wrong that I didn't give the other student the full fifty minutes of learning that I was getting paid to provide him. That was when I got serious about homework-free classrooms and personalized learning.

I decided that in my blended virtual classroom, I wanted my students to commit to working fifty minutes a day… no more and no less. That meant I had to be proactive and provide them with access to different lessons in a class period so that each student would be given exactly what they needed at the exact moment they needed it.

My students quickly and enthusiastically adopted a classroom where they would do all the work for the course during our scheduled time together. By creating individualized learning pathways, I provided each student with exactly what they needed to support their learning. The energy of the room changed as students and parents appreciated a homework-free classroom. My end-of-the-year data supported my work, as the class average for the year was 87 percent, which was the highest it had ever been. I was pleased with that data but thought, "Well, if grades aren't punitively impacted by incomplete homework, then it makes sense." I was more concerned with whether they had mastered the Learning Objectives for the course. I received confirmation that they had when I compiled their final exam data. Our district uses the final exam as a common final summative assessment, carefully crafted to assess mastery of the course objectives. My students earned an 86 percent average, which was the highest any class had ever achieved. Our work was validated, and I have been using the same blended model for my face-to-face instruction ever since.

By building a personalized learning pathway in your LMS, you can create the type of learning that results in engaged students and higher learning outcomes.

Personalized learning based on mastery

By now, you are familiar with the Gradual Release of Responsibility model with the Learning Objective, I Do, We Do, You Do, and Demonstration of Mastery plot points. At each one, learning artifacts provide the instruction and opportunities for learning, and students move forward once they master each phase. If they do not demonstrate mastery of the You Do plot point, they return to the We Do plot point and receive additional instruction using a different instructional strategy before being evaluated again with an alternate You Do assessment. They can access the Demonstration of Mastery plot point after demonstrating their learning on the You Do assessment. See Images 7.1 and 7.2 as a reminder of these simple paths with personalized learning based on mastery.

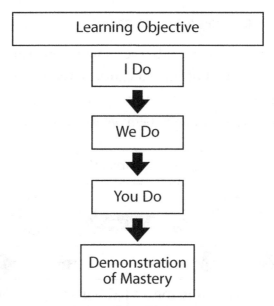

Image 7.1

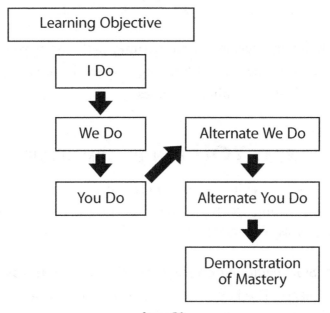

Image 7.2

Personalized learning based on choice

The same model can include even more personalized learning when you add a twist of student choice. Basically, you encourage your students to select the instructional strategies and assessments they believe will help them get to mastery. See Image 7.3.

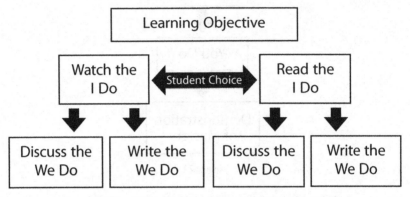

Image 7.3: The Gradual Release of Responsibility model with the added twist of personalized learning through student choice.

By building a personalized learning pathway in your LMS, you can create the type of learning that results in engaged students and higher learning outcomes.

WHAT **YOU** CAN DO TOMORROW

Here are a few first steps to creating personalized student learning paths within the Gradual Release of Responsibility model.

- **Start gathering a variety of artifacts and assessments**. The key to creating individualized learning in a virtual environment is to offer numerous learning artifacts and assessments for you and your students to choose from. List out the ones you already have and search online to add to your collection. Search for the following types of learning artifacts and assessments in your grade level and subject area:

- Virtual discussion questions
- Slow chat prompts
- Collaborative projects
- eLearning platform assignments
- Interactive worksheets and documents
- Interactive videos
- Digital quizzes and surveys
- Digital written prompts
- Video responses

- **Borrow and share**. It can be overwhelming to think about creating so much content, but you just want to gather lots of ideas at first so you can narrow them down to the ones that work best for you. You don't have to generate all the ideas on your own, either. Tap into your PLN and colleagues who may present the lessons differently and can offer fresh ideas, new artifacts, and diverse instructional strategies. Collaborate and share content and ideas to lighten the load for everyone.

- **Look for activities that are interactive and offer a feedback loop.** Students are essentially trying to beat the assessment to get to the next level. If they don't initially pass the level, they will need feedback to redirect their learning, or they will be stuck there. To keep students unstuck, create assessments that provide immediate feedback for the I Do, We Do, and You Do phases. These may be quizzes, surveys, interactive worksheets, documents, and videos with a feedback function. You can use these tools and eLearning programs with both synchronous and asynchronous instruction.

A BLUEPRINT FOR FULL IMPLEMENTATION

STEP 1: Identify the Learning Objective and pick mastery or choice.

When identifying a lesson's Learning Objective, determine whether you will individualize the learning via mastery or student choice. On the mastery path, decide what students need to master and determine a score that proves they have mastered it. For example: *Students will master solving a system of equations by graphing at 85 percent proficiency.* On the choice path, the measurement will vary, depending on how students choose to demonstrate their mastery. You'll want to choose either route as you start planning each lesson because the components will be different with the next steps.

STEP 2: Create 1 Do artifacts.

If you are using mastery to guide your path, then you only need to create one artifact. If you are using choice, create two I Do lessons that use two different instructional strategies so your students can choose to have the instruction delivered to them in the way that they learn best.

STEP 3: Design the We Do activity.

Whether you are using choice or mastery to guide student paths, you'll want at least two learning artifacts with different instructional strategies to support choice and serve as alternative intervention assignments. The We Do plot point is the most critical spot for learning, as it is the area in which the student will interact directly with the teacher to practice learning the content or skill. Utilizing an interactive tool that can be seen by the teacher and the student creates a space where they meet together to amplify learning.

- If the class is synchronous, plan on spending your We Do instruction time providing support and being available to the students when they arrive at the plot point.

- If the class is asynchronous, use an interactive tool that provides preloaded feedback to support learning, like a discussion question with a multiple-choice option.

  ➤ If the student picks the correct answer, they will receive a message reinforcing what they did correctly.

> ➤ If they pick the wrong answer, they will receive
> a message that redirects their thinking and pro-
> vides the correct information so they will learn.

- If you are using choice to drive the learning, then
  you'll create two different activities that utilize two
  learning artifacts, so students can choose which
  works best for them.

STEP 4: Create the You Do assessment.

Once the student completes the We Do activity, they need to demonstrate their understanding of the material or skill. The assessment should be short and provide immediate feedback to the teacher and student regarding what the student does and does not understand.

When using mastery to guide the path, use the data generated from the assessment to determine the next step. Let's go back to the sample Learning Objective—*Students will master solving a system of equations by graphing at 85 percent proficiency*—as an example to guide the next-step options:

- If the student scores 85 percent or higher on
  this assessment, they may move on to the
  Demonstration of Mastery plot point.

- If the student scores below 85 percent, they return
  to the We Do plot and complete the second
  learning artifact that was created as an interventional lesson with a different instructional strategy.

- Once the student has completed the intervention,
  the student will retake the You Do assessment or
  an alternate assessment (teacher's choice).

- If they score 85 percent or higher this time, they will move on to the Demonstration of Mastery plot point.

- If they do not master the goal, the student is instructed to contact the teacher. The teacher then determines what one-on-one intervention the student needs to obtain mastery and provides the intervention until the student can pass the assessment with at least 85 percent accuracy.

When using choice to guide the path, create two different assessments using different strategies. Give your student the option to choose how they would like to demonstrate their learning.

STEP 5: Build a personalized Demonstration of Mastery assessment.

To enter this plot point, students have had to demonstrate mastery of the desired goal and prove they have the skill set to be assessed for a grade. As we covered in Hack 6, the Demonstration of Mastery plot point should be at Depth of Knowledge 4, meaning the student should demonstrate mastery by creating something new. Teachers can create multiple options for the student to demonstrate their mastery of learning. Providing choice on their final summative assessment is an engaging and comprehensive way for the students to demonstrate their learning mastery.

OVERCOMING PUSHBACK

Designing individualized instruction can seem like an extra layer of challenge for teachers, so, understandably, some teachers may resist it before they fully understand the value to their students. Here are two types of resistance and how to respond.

Personalized learning seems like an awful lot of work. Building personalized learning requires a tremendous amount of planning, building, and adherence to the plot points of the Gradual Release of Responsibility model, especially in virtual or flex teaching environments. At first glance, it may appear to be more work than it is worth. Educators are working to solve issues of inequity, including those brought to light during pandemic teaching, while students are entering our classrooms with more diverse needs that we can't possibly predict. Putting in the time and effort to create personalized learning paths based on mastery and choice will help ensure that your teaching meets each student's unique needs. The good news is that you only have to build the process once, and then it repeats itself in a sustainable way.

Why should I personalize learning if my students and I will be assessed on standardized tests? Personalized learning does not change the *what* of learning. It changes the *how*. Students will likely still be learning the standards-based curriculum, and your Learning Objective will be based on your standards. However, if you personalize learning for mastery, then the "how long" part gets personalized. If you personalize learning for choice, then the "how it's taught" part gets personalized. Both accomplish the same goal: student mastery of the Learning Objective.

THE HACK IN ACTION

Colleen Haag is an award-winning eighth grade science teacher and instructional coach who creates personalized learning for her middle school students using Canvas's MasteryPaths content builder. She was recognized for her personalized learning strategies when she won the 2020 Canvas Educator of the Year Award.

She says, "I started using MasteryPaths a few years ago after I realized that some students in my academic class had completed their work faster than the other students. I was very surprised when I asked the class who would like to be challenged. A few kids wanted to complete some enrichment work and accepted the challenge."

She remembers how the students loved the opportunity to use their class time to continue their learning with additional activities that they could choose. She quickly learned that by utilizing MasteryPaths, she could also provide more support to students who needed more time to understand concepts. She began using it to create paths for remediation with follow-up assessments to ensure mastery of the Learning Objective. Personalized learning has become a staple of her instruction ever since.

"I use MasteryPaths in my class to provide my students with choice, differentiation, and mastery learning. I teach around 130 students that range from learning support to students with GIEPs."

For example, her curriculum covers physics and chemistry that require strong math skills. She builds a MasteryPath for her students based on their math skills.

"I have students in each class that range in their math ability from pre-algebra all the way up to geometry. Students are often reluctant or embarrassed to let the class know which math they are in. With MasteryPaths, students are able to select their math level, and they are assigned different work in those units without anyone else in the class knowing."

She was pleased to see that her efforts to personalize the learning based on student ability were meeting the needs of her students, and she was excited when students began requesting an opportunity to push their learning by accessing the harder paths. They were motivated to try harder work.

Here's a brief description of the MasteryPaths function in Canvas; other Learning Management Systems may offer a similar program. Canvas uses the data obtained from the assignment to determine each student's next assignment. It can best be described as "choose your own adventure." However, the student's score dictates the next leg of the adventure. For example, a teacher creates an assignment and selects MasteryPaths, then creates pathways by adding additional assignments. If a student scores seven to ten points, they go to Path A, which contains a Path A assignment. If they score six points and below, they go to Path B, which contains a Path B assignment. The teacher determines the number of paths and how to use the data to assign paths. This option allows teachers to creatively personalize student learning by using data to automatically determine the next assignment without the student checking with the teacher for direction.

Before you try out personalized learning, Haag advises you first come up with a reason for differentiating. Determine if you are differentiating to provide choice, remediation, or enrichment. "Start with a quiz as the trigger to start the MasteryPath throughout the assignment," Haag says. "Then sketch out the three different pathways that you would like students to venture through. Create the work for those pathways."

Her final advice is to always try out the paths in student view to determine if they provide the personalized learning you intended.

Like Haag, you can use technology to disrupt the space-time continuum of learning and provide personalized experiences that benefit your students' learning and their confidence. Combining the philosophy of personalized learning and embedding it into the plot points of the Gradual Release of Responsibility, teachers can meet the needs and interests of all of their virtual learning students.

Providing every student with exactly what they need, at the exact time they need it, and for the exact amount of time they need it seems like an educational pipe dream. Technology coupled with strong pedagogy will allow teachers to alter the space-time continuum and make this educational dream of equity a reality. By using the Gradual Release of Responsibility and building learning paths based on mastery or choice, teachers can personalize student learning and allow all of their students to be in different learning spots at the same time. Although it requires a tremendous amount of planning, once the paths are built, students will benefit from having every second of class meet their unique needs. They will no longer have to wait for others to catch up or have to use personal time to finish their work—and this change will result in authentic learning equity.

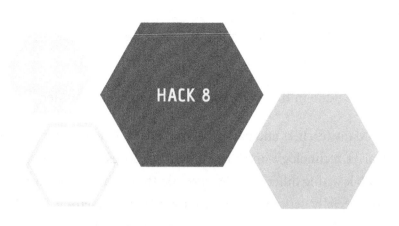

SUPPORT SPECIAL EDUCATION STUDENTS
Use Technological Least Restrictive Environments

One who seeks equity must do equity.
—UNKNOWN

THE PROBLEM: It's challenging to modify lessons for special education students in a virtual setting

EVERY CLASSROOM HAS students with learning differences that need support, and it can be an extra challenge for teachers to provide accommodations and modifications in a virtual classroom. Consider these stats:

- One in five students has dyslexia.

- One in six students has dysgraphia.

- One in ten has ADD/ADHD.

- One in fifty-four has autism spectrum disorder.

Many teachers and parents do not know enough about the potential of technology and virtual best practices to support students with learning differences. As a result, they do not know to advocate for specially designed instruction in the virtual setting. This lack of knowledge results in individualized education plans (IEPs) that fall short of meeting the virtual learning needs of the student.

When a student's teachers and guardians develop an IEP, they identify student learning weaknesses and create a plan to support the child's learning goals. They determine what modifications and accommodations can help students reach their goals so they can receive Free Appropriate Public Education (FAPE) in the least restrictive environment.

Following the Gradual Release of Responsibility model with the adoption of personalized learning pathways can help teachers modify their content to meet the goals of their students. Still, they need the technology to provide accommodations to the instruction and assessments. Teachers can support their special education students by substituting existing face-to-face specially designed instruction (SDIs) with virtual specially designed instruction.

THE HACK: Support special education students

In a face-to-face classroom, the IEP often requires a second teacher to help implement the specially designed instruction. While it serves a purpose, receiving this kind of support can be problematic for certain students, as learned helplessness can result from students having to rely on adults for their learning needs.

Switching to a virtual learning environment creates an outstanding opportunity for some special education students to obtain more learning autonomy that is not easily achieved in a face-to-face setting. When used appropriately and with certain students, technology can provide the required support even without a second classroom teacher. This allows special education students to truly learn in the least restrictive environment.

Unfortunately, because of the novelty of virtual learning, parents and teachers are unfamiliar with how technology can support students with learning differences, and they do not know how to advocate for appropriate interventions. As a result, teachers and parents will use what they know about face-to-face specially designed instruction and find a virtual workaround. Although IEPs are intended to be personalized, common specially designed instructions exist that teachers can fairly easily substitute in a virtual setting.

WHAT YOU CAN DO TOMORROW

- **Look for common IEP themes**. Review your students' IEPs and identify the most common specially designed instruction. Special education students often require the same type of support, so finding themes will help guide you as you find virtual substitutions to meet their needs.

- **See if your LMS has built-in supportive features**. Investigate the features of your LMS to see if it can provide options for specially designed instruction.

Many LMS systems do. If so, compare the features to your students' common IEP themes to see if the built-in capabilities can help support most of your students and their needs.

- **Join a special education PLN.** Hop on Twitter or Facebook to collaborate with colleagues and find resources for teaching special education students virtually. Numerous special education groups are on social media, and you can find them by searching for "special education" to access the groups or connect with specific followers. Online collaboration among teachers facing the same challenges can offer great ideas on using technology in innovative ways to support all of your students' needs.

- **Brainstorm with tech coaches.** Connect with your district technology coaches to brainstorm ways to meet your special education students' needs. Don't be shy about reaching out for help, as they will have insight into programs, apps, and extensions that can help support your students.

A BLUEPRINT FOR FULL IMPLEMENTATION

After you have identified your most common specially designed instructions (see the first bullet under the What You Can Do Tomorrow section), compare them to the following common SDIs and consider implementing these virtual substitution hacks to support every student's learning.

STEP 1: Hack the SDI "read-aloud options."

Students with dyslexia or others who struggle with reading will benefit from having their text read to them. Whether it is a worksheet or a textbook, they should be able to access a digital tool to support their reading. The majority of devices have built-in accessibility features that provide text-to-speech support. In addition, multiple extensions and apps can support this learning need. Teaching students to either access the accessibility features or the app/extension will satisfy the need to have text read to them.

STEP 2: Hack the SDI "teacher will scribe."

Students with dysgraphia who struggle with handwriting or composition will benefit from having someone, or in this case, something, to write for them. Accessibility features to support speech-to-text, often called dictation tools, are built-in to devices. Apps and extensions also meet this need. Work with students to find a dictation tool they can easily use to meet this need.

STEP 3: Hack the SDI "chunking of directions."

For students with dyslexia, ADD/ADHD, or autism spectrum disorder, following directions can be challenging. In a digital setting, instructions that involve the student having to understand what they should do, where they should do it, and in what order requires strong executive functioning skills. Teachers have found that chunking directions in the face-to-face setting has helped support students with low executive functioning. However, given the complexity and independent nature of a digital environment, chunking directions will be more complex.

If you are providing written directions, split up the directions into manageable chunks. For example, as we covered in Hack 2, use a template to communicate directions consistently. This need is amplified when working with students who have learning differences. You can create a template for the day or class activities by following a format that includes all the information and resources for the student to be successful.

Begin by labeling your module or folder by the date instead of the name of the assignment or subject area. This makes it easy for the student to determine which posting they should access. Have a designated spot in your module or folder that houses the day's announcements, directions, links, or attachments all in one place so the student doesn't have to click out to a separate page or site to get the directions or materials necessary to be successful.

Here are ideas for how to provide instructions via a simple template format:

- Start with a greeting in which the teacher tries to make a personal connection with the student.

- Chunk all directions, write them simply, and number them so students are not overburdened with too many words to process or do not have to rely on their problem-solving skills to figure out what they need to do.

- Hyperlink all external links in the directions and teach students to identify hyperlinks so they can access the resources from the directions.

- Include all attachments in the module/folder on the directions page so they don't have to go to a different portion of the LMS to access the necessary materials.

If you choose to use video to provide directions, please split it up into manageable parts based on the video's purpose. For example, if you provide three steps to follow, then post three videos. In addition, title and number the videos so the student can access the information they need without having to re-watch the entire video.

STEP 4: Hack the SDI "check for understanding."

It's a challenge in a virtual setting to check for understanding of students who process information differently, such as those with dyslexia, ADD/ADHD, or autism spectrum disorder, but it's a solvable challenge. It requires the teacher to plan ahead, invest time learning new tools, and go about it in a thoughtful, efficient, and well-executed way.

To ensure each student is progressing in their learning, check for understanding in these three areas:

1. Does the student understand the directions?

2. Does the student understand the material being taught?

3. Does the student understand the feedback they are receiving?

Digital tools are our allies when it comes to assessing student understanding. Use them to help perform front-loaded checks, real-time checks, and back-loaded checks. Here's how:

- **Front-loaded check:** The teacher will develop an assessment that quickly checks for understanding and upload it before the module is accessible to the student. Front-loaded checks, while they require more planning and execution, are the most successful strategy for checking for understanding because they immediately notify the teacher and the student if the student hasn't mastered the understanding and will need an intervention before doing additional work. This can be done with numerous assessment tools.

Teachers can create quizzes in their LMS or other apps to determine if a student understands the directions, content, and teacher feedback. The quiz can include multiple-choice questions, matching, or true-and-false questions, but for efficiency, it must have the capability to automatically grade and provide instant feedback to the teacher and the student. For example, a teacher can provide directions for the day on a content page. Immediately after, they can post a true-or-false quiz and assess if the student understands what is expected. If possible, choose a tool with a "provide feedback for incorrect answers" option as a great way to provide redirection and feedback to a student when they answer incorrectly.

- **Real-time check:** The teacher will communicate with the student in real time to determine if the student has a mastery understanding of the information. Teachers can use interactive presentation tools, content-specific interactive tools, and interactive videos to assess understanding as the student is learning the material. Assessments like polls, quizzes, and open-ended discussion questions can be embedded into the presentation, content-specific activity, or video. As soon as the student submits their response, the teacher will have an instant snapshot of the student's understanding of the material. As in the front-loaded check, the teacher can select the "provide feedback for incorrect answers" option.

Digital tools that give the teacher access to the student's desktop or screen are also great ways for the teacher to check for understanding. These tools allow teachers to monitor their students' work in real time and then provide feedback right at the point when it is needed.

Tools that provide discussion boards and back-channel chats can also be tapped for the teacher to check for understanding by engaging in an online conversation with the student. This is similar to how you engage with students in person to determine if they understand what they are supposed to be doing and learning.

- **Back-loaded check:** The teacher will determine student understanding through the action or inaction of the students. Then the teacher can modify instruction after the assessment to determine further instruction, often resulting in additional instructional support with extended time or an alternate assignment. Back-loaded checks, while easiest for the teacher to develop because they are reactive and require no planning, are the least successful for students. This strategy requires the student to work without an assurance that they understand what is expected of them and could result in wasted time because they spent the class doing something incorrectly. Because the intervention occurs after the student has already invested time and effort into doing the work, the student can frustrate easily and it can trigger past learning traumas that make any meaningful learning difficult.

STEP 5: Hack the SDI "pre-teaching, reteaching, and study guides."

For students who require pre-teaching, reteaching, and study guides, video is an excellent way to access the material without relying on their literacy skills, which may be weak. With the creative use of a presentation tool and a screencasting tool, teachers can create videos of their lectures, worksheets, or study guides and make them accessible at the start of the unit for pre-teaching, before second-chance learning in the form of reteaching, and as a study guide before an assessment.

- **For pre-teaching,** create a short video that introduces the student to the new language or concepts they will need to master to successfully participate in the planned lesson.

- **For reteaching,** this requires a more in-depth presentation as you review the key concepts and skills necessary for the student to achieve mastery. Here's how you can accomplish this:

> Use a presentation tool to create the visual image that you will present.

> Choose a screencasting tool and record yourself while displaying the presentation you created.

> Make your video accessible to the student to review before beginning the unit.

- **For study guides,** you can turn a worksheet or notes into a video, resulting in a multisensory experience in which the student can see and hear the content. This especially helps students with learning differences who may struggle with learning from the visual-only content of a worksheet or notes, especially if they have a weakness in reading. The student can replay the video as often as needed to help master the material. Here's how you can accomplish this:

  > Show a complete study guide with correct answers.

  > Scan a study guide into a PDF.

  > Use the snipping tool to chunk the questions and post them on slides in a presentation tool.

  > Choose your screencasting tool and record yourself both asking and answering the questions.

> Make your video accessible to the student before the test so they can watch it as often as needed before taking an assessment.

You can make a huge difference in the lives of your most vulnerable students when you take the time to learn new ways that technology can support their understanding.

STEP 6: **Guide students to follow these best practices to stay organized.**

All students, whether or not they have IEPs, can benefit by learning and following best practices to stay organized and on track. Here are three ideas to share with your students, especially special education students, around digital organization.

- **Graphic organizers:** Students with executive functioning issues or dysgraphia may require a graphic organizer to help manage their writing. In a digital setting, graphic organizers can add depth to instruction that a traditional paper graphic organizer can't offer. For example, teachers can support areas of weakness by hyperlinking definitions or examples to help students learn a particular concept. To support composition, teachers can hyperlink videos of direct instruction about composition to help students develop the skill.

- **Assignment books:** Many students who need help managing their homework can benefit by using an assignment book. All LMSs have a task management function to support student learning. The task management system will either be in the form of a to-do list or a calendar that can replace an assignment book. Teachers need to make sure they are properly labeling their assignments so they register on the student's task management tool. Also, teachers need to work with the students to develop a routine to check the task management tool daily, as they would with a paper assignment book.

- **Bookmarks and desktop shortcuts:** In virtual learning, students no longer have to worry about keeping track of papers, folders, textbooks, and supplies. However, managing multiple digital pieces of content can be a challenge. Teaching students to bookmark or create desktop shortcuts is a valuable digital literacy skill that can assist anyone with organization. For example, teachers can help students organize their work by showing them how to bookmark the important links, materials, and sites they visit often, so they can more quickly access and manage their materials.

OVERCOMING PUSHBACK

Special education students in the United States are entitled to a Free Appropriate Public Education, regardless of setting. Shifting to a virtual environment does not change our students' federally protected right. Teachers are tasked with providing specially designed virtual instruction so they can teach all students with equity. While the work is challenging, it matters. You may have felt or heard the following concerns.

I don't know enough about technology to support special education students in a virtual setting. You don't need to be a tech guru to support students with learning differences. Embrace the requirement and start by implementing the hacks described in this chapter. As you become more comfortable with your virtual instruction, you will begin to develop a mastery understanding of your instructional strategies and the tools you've selected to implement them. You will understand how you can make a huge difference in the lives of your most vulnerable students when you take the time to learn new ways that technology can support their understanding.

It's easier for my co-teacher or support staff to provide the accommodation than it is for me to invest in learning a new tool. All of this is true. It is much easier to ask a second adult in the room to read a test to a student instead of investigating and downloading the best text-to-speech app and teaching a student to use it. However, that does not create the least restrictive environment. When you choose to bring a second person into the student's learning, you take away the student's independence and tell them their success depends on receiving help. It is imperative that teachers do everything in their power to ensure that all of their students can be empowered learners, capable of independently navigating their education, despite any learning differences they may have.

THE HACK IN ACTION

As a special needs parent, I am invested in and passionate about using technology to knock down education barriers for special needs students. My oldest son, Jake, was born with a physical disability. By second grade, we had learned that he also had multiple learning disabilities, including dyslexia, dysgraphia, dyspraxia, ADHD, and anxiety. As you might imagine, school has always been difficult for him. However, his supportive and innovative teachers have created the least restrictive environment by using technology to support his learning differences. The work didn't come easy at first.

In 2015 when he was beginning fourth grade, I asked the district to provide him with a Chromebook to support his learning needs. He was the first student in the district to be issued one, and his teachers had no idea what to do with this device. Fortunately, I had just completed a school year in which I piloted a Chromebook initiative and had seen firsthand the transformational power of these magical little devices for nondisabled students. I knew it would be a game-changer for my special education son who struggled to read and write independently.

That first year, I trained all of his teachers and taught my son how to use the Chromebook. We began with the text-to-speech function. He simply had to speak to the computer, and it translated his complex thoughts into correctly spelled, legibly written words. This gave him the freedom to finally be able to articulate himself without shame or embarrassment. Then we focused on text-to-speech and figured out how to get all of his worksheets and textbooks into digital form so the Chromebook could read to him. That eliminated his need to rely on another human to read for him.

I developed collaborative relationships with his teachers, often showing them something new they could do with the device or an app to support his learning. With each new academic challenge he faced, his teachers and I would brainstorm how the device could support his learning, always with the ultimate goal of providing him independence. Our goal was to avoid learned helplessness so he could be an empowered student capable of independent learning.

I've taken what I have learned and presented it at state-level and national conferences, helping other teachers learn how to support their special education students by providing them with the least restrictive environment.

Kelly Merritt is a high school reading specialist and English teacher who is creating the least restrictive environment by empowering her students. She provides remediation for students with dyslexia and dysgraphia. Merritt has the incredible responsibility of providing evidence-based and specially designed instruction to support their learning needs and ensure her students are mastering their goals. She finds that virtual learning can exploit her students' learning differences.

"My students have various processing issues that impact their ability to learn virtually. Focus and attention are the most pervasive issues, but listening comprehension and visual tracking also impair their abilities to follow directions or even properly implement the steps needed to accomplish any task independently."

She says she finds that weaknesses in executive functioning can make accessing the learning difficult because following directions without face-to-face support can be a challenge. "The student may hear the directions, understand the directions, but then incorrectly implement the directions, and the teacher does not even realize until well after the assignment is turned in," Merritt explains. She points out that waiting until after an assignment is turned in to determine that a student couldn't follow the directions has dire consequences on student learning. "This compounds the skill deficits and pushes students further away from being on grade level with their peers. Lost time with my students may never be made up."

Merritt has found that the specially designed instructions that have been put into IEPs are not aligned with a virtual setting; they need teachers to adapt them to fit. "SDIs like preferential seating, written directions, and graphic organizers are no longer valid means of supporting these students. Other means need to be put into place, but often the student and the teacher do not know what these accommodations could be in a virtual learning platform."

To support her special needs students in virtual classes, Merritt has adapted the existing SDIs into the technology. For example, to support students with a weakness in following directions, she creates directions that are easy to follow. She also chunks assignments into manageable pieces. "I repeat, restate, and reinforce the steps during synchronous learning to ensure my students understand what I'm asking them to do."

Aware that once the asynchronous meeting ends, she will no longer be able to provide teacher-centered support, she records the directions so her students can listen to them repeatedly.

Merritt checks for understanding by using a program called **GoGuardian**, which gives her visual access to her students' desktops in real time so she can see what they are working on. "I use programs like **GoGuardian** to track students during class time to make sure they understand the directions, are staying focused, and to identify when a student is making an error. Correcting their errors in real time is more effective than waiting until they've submitted it to be graded."

She uses the chat feature to provide redirection as well as praise and encouragement. "I also periodically check in with all students to comment on their progress and give them a thumbs-up to let them know I see the good work they are doing. I find it's good for me to see and comment on the students who are staying on-task as opposed to just focusing on students who are losing their way."

She is one example of a teacher who uses technology to create virtual specially designed instructions to meet the executive functioning needs of students. Merritt demonstrates that special education students can learn and progress in a virtual setting when teachers invest time in the worthy work of wrangling the technology to support all of their students.

Technology has afforded schools an awesome opportunity to create equity by offering the least restrictive environment to provide support for students with learning differences. Teachers are faced with the awesome responsibility of learning the technology to provide specially designed instruction that will generate learning independence for our most vulnerable students. Get started by identifying the most common face-to-face specially designed instruction and follow the hacks in this chapter to adapt them and empower your special education students.

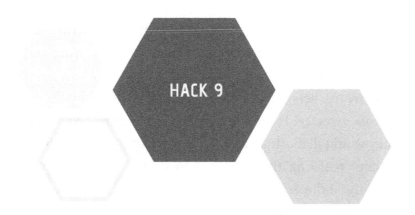

ECONOMIZE YOUR EFFICIENCY

Choose the Least Amount of Work, In the Least Amount of Time, for the Best Possible Learning Outcomes

Even miracles take a little time.
—FAIRY GODMOTHER IN *CINDERELLA*, BY WALT DISNEY

THE PROBLEM: Teachers' lives are consumed with planning, building, and grading

THE EXISTENTIAL CRISIS facing education is teachers leaving the profession due to burnout … and that was before COVID-19. The crippling amount of time and work associated with planning, executing, and assessing student learning is the primary antagonist. Seasoned teachers know that the key to longevity is efficiency: figuring out how to do the least amount of work, in the least amount of time, for the best possible learning outcomes. Transitioning from face-to-face to virtual learning exploits the work and time associated with planning and preparing lessons.

Many teachers found themselves overwhelmed by the amount of work associated with the first step of planning a virtual lesson. They would dedicate hours of precious time planning the lesson without realizing they still had to devote time to execute the learning and assess student understanding ... just to do it all over again the next day!

It doesn't have to be that way. Armed with a strong pedagogy and virtual instructional and assessment strategies, teachers can economize their efficiency by making instructional decisions that hit the sweet spot of the least amount of work, in the least amount of time, for the best possible learning outcomes. Learning to make thrifty decisions in how you spend your time in the various stages of planning will give you control of your efficiency and, ultimately, control of your burnout. (For more about overcoming burnout and going from isolated to empowered, read *Hacking Teacher Burnout* by Amber Harper.)

THE HACK: Economize your efficiency

When you take control over your educational work time, you will be intentional about how you spend every minute, and you will be efficient. First, set your work hours. How much time, ideally, do you plan to spend on work each week? Then divide the number of minutes into planning time and instruction time. I'll walk you through this process in the A Blueprint for Full Implementation section.

Your lesson planning should consist of the following factors:

- How much planning time will it take to develop the learning artifact or assessment?

- How much class time will it take to implement the learning or assessment?

- What is the shelf life of the lesson and assessment?

When you begin to value efficiency and make instructional decisions based on the merging of efficiency and learning outcomes, you will find that you don't have to spend hours upon hours planning and developing lessons. By following the Gradual Release of Responsibility model, you set a game plan for building student learning, which will save you time when determining what pedagogy to use. Because you have strategized your instructional strategies and mastered the tools associated with them, you can eliminate the time it takes to ponder which strategy and tool to use. Making decisions about when and how to use assessment will be easier and more efficient because you have assessed your assessment. Using this knowledge for your planning will help you make informed decisions about how you spend your time.

WHAT **YOU** CAN DO TOMORROW

- **Assess your current reward/risk**. Review your current instructional strategies or assessment decisions and determine if the time associated with making and implementing the learning artifact or assessment is worth your investment of minutes. Ask yourself if the reward (student learning) is worth the time you risk (planning and teaching) or if there's room to lower your risk and increase the reward.

- **Create a data table to support your planning**. In the data table, identify the GRR plot points (Learning Objective, I Do, We Do, Alternate We Do, You Do, Alternate You Do, and Demonstration of Mastery) and determine which instructional strategies, assessments, and tools you could potentially use for any lesson. Having the data table will speed up your decision-making process about planning.

- **Sketch out a future lesson**. Using the data table you just created, rough out a future lesson and focus on making decisions that will effectively use your planning and instructional time.

A BLUEPRINT FOR FULL IMPLEMENTATION

Utilizing my Gradual Release of Responsibility template (without mastery or choice paths), I will walk you through my decision-making process with one lesson as an example and show you the data table I use to economize my efficiency. You can apply this example to your situation. Note that your goal will be different from mine, and the time you allot to planning and instruction will be different from mine, depending on factors such as the grade level you teach and your school's schedule. My goal: To create a five-day lesson that applies to all learning environments without having to work outside of my contractual day and without having to make my students complete homework.

Each week, I start fresh with 275 planning minutes and 275 instructional minutes. To reach my goal, I need to create learning artifacts and assessments that require less than 275 minutes of planning and 275 minutes of instructional time.

I created the following simple data table (see Image 9.1) as a guide for decision-making. With each lesson, I can assess its efficiency and determine if the planning, instructional time, and shelf life make it a practical plan. Follow along with the steps in my example and create your own data table with one of your lessons.

PLOT POINT	Instructional Strategy	TOOL	SHELF LIFE	PLAN TIME	CLASS TIME
I Do					
We Do					
You Do Assessment					
Demonstration of Mastery					

Image 9.1: My data table, ready to be filled in with the details of a lesson so I can evaluate its efficiency.

STEP 1: Begin with the Learning Objective.

For this lesson, the Learning Objective for my students was to identify the five principles of existentialism in their pop culture.

STEP 2: Develop the I Do.

Previously, I used an entire class period to lecture about the five principles. However, I was inefficient in my delivery, as I would often go too deep into the principles or fall into an off-topic rabbit hole discussion. I would like to be more efficient in my lecture delivery.

I decided to create five teacher-centered videos, with each one no longer than five minutes. I used Google Slides and Screencastify and then used Canvas to hold the learning artifact so the students could access it for their asynchronous learning. The planning time was quite extensive, and I anticipated ninety minutes. I knew I would spend time creating Google Slides to provide the visual content for the video, and it would take a minimum of thirty minutes to record the five videos. However, I was pleased with the thought of only using half a class period to deliver the content, and because the shelf life is forever, I will not have to use any planning time to prepare future lessons on this topic. The risk associated with using two hours to plan the lecture seems worth it because the reward of having no future planning for a more efficient lesson is worth it to me. See the first completed row in Image 9.2.

PLOT POINT	Instructional Strategy	TOOL	SHELF LIFE	PLAN TIME	CLASS TIME
I Do	Teacher-Centered Video	Slides, Screencastify, Canvas	X	90 min.	30 min.
We Do	Slow Chat	Canvas	X	5 min.	55 min.
You Do Assessment	Multiple Choice Quiz w/ Automatic Feedback	Canvas	X	90 min.	30 min.
Demonstration of Mastery	Student-Centered Screencast	Slides, Screencastify, Storyboard That	X	70 min.	90 min.

Image 9.2: My completed data table for the lesson on the
five principles of existentialism in pop culture.

STEP 3: Plan the We Do.

When I taught this lesson in person, I included a fifty-five-minute student-centered class discussion to give them a chance to use the new terminology and deepen their understanding with each other. At the same time, I provided feedback and additional instruction when needed. In this example, I feel comfortable using the same amount of class time for the students to practice. I don't have any modifications I would like to make other than finding a way to accomplish the same student interaction in any setting.

I decided to use Canvas's Discussion Board to create a slow chat for the students to participate in a student-centered synchronous discussion. The prep time is minimal at five minutes since I only have to post the discussion questions in Canvas. Once I created the questions for the We Do, I can use them forever. See the second completed row in Image 9.2.

STEP 4: Create an assessment for the You Do.

I want my students to be able to define the principles and be able to identify them in their pop culture. However, I want them to prove, first, that they can see the principles in pop culture before I send them out on their own to find examples. I support their learning by providing examples and giving them the chance to work on their analysis of the principles.

Using Canvas's Quiz Tool, I can provide students with multiple songs that represent each principle. They have the task of figuring out which principle is represented by which song. Here's how I created the nonpunitive assessment:

- I pull several samples of lyrics for students to analyze to determine which principle the lyrics represent.

- I create a multiple-choice assessment that automatically grades their responses and provides real-time feedback for correct and incorrect answers. The benefit of using a self-grading assessment is that it will allow me to quickly scan through the scores to determine if they are ready to move on to the Demonstration of Mastery plot point.

- If they have not mastered the material, I choose to reteach specific students or address the class as a whole before the summative assessment. Using question data, I provide additional targeted instruction to support learning.

- I reassess using the same assessment until they have demonstrated mastery.

Creating an interactive assessment that self-grades and provides feedback takes a lot of planning time. I estimate about ninety minutes to create it and thirty minutes for the students to complete it. It's time-consuming to build, but it's worth it because it provides me with important data quickly and can be used repeatedly. See the third completed row in Image 9.2.

In virtual environments, teachers and students benefit from a structured pedagogy and using efficiency to help solve problems.

STEP 5: Design an assessment for Demonstration of Mastery.

In this final step, now that all of the instructional heavy lifting is complete, students will be charged with the task of making their learning visible by creating something out of nothing. To help them demonstrate mastery of the Learning Objective, I assigned them to create a screencast that shows their ability to define and identify the five principles of existentialism in their pop culture.

Existentialism and Pop Culture

Now that you have learned about principles of existentialism, and identified them in music, you're now charged with the task of finding these five principles in your own world.

Please use the attached slideshow template and do the following:

Step 1) Identify the five principles of existentialism

Step 2) Find examples of each principle in your pop-culture which can include your music, books, art, film, and social media

Step 3) Creatively display your sample with the principle in the slideshow

Step 4) Use screencastify to create a two minute screencast in which you define each principle and explain how your sample represents your principle

Please see the attached report for information regarding how you will be graded.

Image 9.3: This screenshot shows my instructions to students on how to demonstrate their mastery and meet the Learning Objective for a lesson on existentialism and pop culture.

The planning time will be minimal, about ten minutes, as I simply have to create the slideshow template and post the directions in Canvas. The bulk of the work associated with this task will be in watching the screencasts and manually grading the work using the rubric. By putting a time limit on the project, I can control the time it takes to grade—about sixty minutes. I anticipate it will take about ninety minutes of class time for the students to complete the activity. See the completed table in Image 9.2.

My objective, again, was to economize my efficiency by creating a lesson that would not require more than the allotted 275 planning minutes and 275 instructional minutes and could be used in all learning environments.

After adding up the minutes in my data table for this lesson, I will use 255 planning minutes and 205 instructional minutes. That gives me a cushion of twenty additional planning minutes in case something doesn't go as planned. A fifty-five-minute cushion will provide additional support to students who may need more time to obtain mastery of their learning. In addition, all of the learning artifacts and assessments have a shelf life past this year, and I can use them again without any planning. That means when I use this lesson again, it will prove to be incredibly efficient. I will earn back all of the planning time I invested by creating the assignment.

OVERCOMING PUSHBACK

As teachers transition from new teachers to master teachers, their time spent on planning decreases. With time and experience, they develop an ebb and flow to their instruction that requires very little time lamenting about all of the instructional details. The ebb and flow went out of whack when we shifted to a virtual setting. Everyone turned back into a new teacher, and planning, once again, became a critical part of the instructional day. Unfortunately, planning time must compete with the actual time it takes to build digital content. In virtual environments, teachers and students benefit from a structured pedagogy and using efficiency to help solve problems. Yet, the following common pushbacks persist.

Too much structure takes away from my ability to teach. Unfortunately, the days of walking into a classroom and simply winging it by lecturing throughout a class period are over. Virtual learning, whether blended, hybrid, distance, or flex, requires planning and thoughtful assessment. To be successful, every aspect of learning must be intentional because what has always worked in a face-to-face classroom no longer has a place in a virtual classroom. The setting has changed, which means everything that used to work has to be reassessed and thoughtfully planned. Teaching with a structured curriculum makes sense in a virtual environment.

I feel like I'm a bad teacher when I rely on technology to do my job. I have often heard this from colleagues who feel a natural discomfort when they begin to rely on technology to help out with some of the heavy lifting of teaching. For example, I worked with a social studies teacher who felt like she was cheating if she didn't spend the entire fifty-five minutes of her synchronous course lecturing about the material in the chapter. Each day, she would then tell the students to read the chapter in the eBook, which covered the same material as the lecture, on their own and fill out the interactive worksheet that provided real-time feedback at the end of the chapter. I asked her how long it would take the students to read the chapter on their own. She said it wouldn't take more than twenty minutes. I followed up by asking how long it would take to have them fill out the worksheet. She said ten minutes. I asked if any material was in the chapter that was not in the lecture. She said no, she based her lectures on exactly what was in the chapter. I then asked the obvious question: "Why are you lecturing?"

She explained that it was her job to tell the students about what happened. I suggested that her job was to make sure the students learned the content in the chapter, and she agreed that was the primary goal. Then I started doing the math and used the Gradual Release to show her how she could be more efficient in her planning. I explained she was using two I Dos by lecturing and using the book. The We Do was the interactive worksheet requiring ten minutes. So, that lesson cost her fifty-five minutes of instructional time and thirty minutes of the students' personal time. A total of eighty-five minutes were used to obtain the Learning Objective.

If she used the chapter in the eBook as the I Do and the interactive worksheet for the We Do, she would shave down her in-class instructional time to thirty minutes. Essentially, she would achieve the same goal with thirty minutes of class time as she would with fifty-five minutes of class time and thirty minutes of homework. The best part yet … no homework for the students. Her initial comment was: "But then I'll feel like a bad teacher." My response: "That's not possible because not only will you be achieving your Learning Objectives, but you will be doing it without assigning homework. Your administration will be happy the learning is occurring, and your students and their parents will be grateful that you didn't have to use any time at home to complete it." The technology can create a win-win-win.

THE HACK IN ACTION

Before I became a virtual teacher, I held strong opinions about what good instruction looked like. I subscribed to the compliance model in which class time was spent with all of my students sitting at their desks, listening to me talk about whatever I was teaching them that day. The last few minutes of class were for them to start their homework by practicing whatever skill or concept I had taught. Whatever they didn't finish, I would assign as homework. The next day, I would begin by checking to see that they completed their homework, which many did not. If they did, sometimes it was oddly similar to their best friend's homework.

Then I would launch into my teacher-centered instruction and repeat the process the next day and every day for the rest of the school year.

Today, I cringe at the inefficiency of my past teaching. I was so bad at making efficient planning decisions that I would require the students to use their personal time at home to help me out because I couldn't figure out how to do it all in one class period.

Virtual teaching forced me to develop new, dynamic, and efficient instructional and assessment strategies. I began adopting those strategies into my face-to-face class and created a blended classroom in which we did most of our learning following the same pedagogy I had adopted in my fully virtual course. To my surprise, I became a much more efficient teacher. So much so that I no longer needed to assign homework. I completed all the tasks associated with learning during the class time and created a homework-free classroom. My educational evolution resulted in more efficient use of class time and my time. My students became homework-free ... and so did I!

When I started working more efficiently, I was worried that I might be missing something. I feared that because we were spending less time working, the students weren't learning. However, that fear was replaced with affirmation when I calculated the final grades for the school year. I was thrilled to calculate an 87 percent class average—the highest class average I had ever recorded. While I was excited about the number, I was still a little suspect that perhaps my grading was biased and the average wasn't based on actual learning outcomes. That changed after I calculated the final exam. Our district uses a common grade level final exam based on the state standards for the grade level. My students scored an 86 percent class average, which was well above any final exam average I had ever scored before. That cemented my belief in the value of efficiency.

Using the Gradual Release of Responsibility helps teachers create a structured pedagogy that supports student learning, and it also aids in planning. Although it requires an initial investment of time, you can efficiently design lessons and tests with timeless shelf lives. As you begin developing and acquiring digital learning artifacts and assessments, your planning time will be drastically cut, allowing you to use your planning time to assess. By economizing your efficiency, you will have mastered the art of the least amount of work, in the least amount of time, for the best possible learning outcomes.

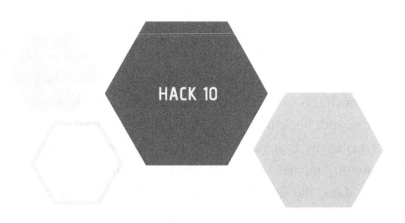

FALL IN LOVE WITH DIGITAL LITERACY

Harness Technology to Make Teaching Easier

Any sufficiently advanced technology is indistinguishable from magic.
—ARTHUR C. CLARKE

THE PROBLEM: Teachers need hacky ways to make technology work for them

WAS SEVEN YEARS old when I proudly announced that I wanted to be a teacher. I was inspired by my awesome second grade teacher, Mrs. Yocum, who would sing the spelling of words to help us remember how to spell them. This inspiration was coupled with the thrill I got when I would be permitted to write on the chalkboard. I was set on becoming a teacher and one day being in charge of my own classroom. However, I did not realize there was so much more to teaching than singing and chalk. I had no idea how much this career choice would consume my life, my time, my energy, and, I might as well add, my heart and soul.

During my first year of teaching, I was overwhelmed by the numerous menial tasks that would suck up my time and, on some days, the joy of my classroom. Before I embraced technology, my workday began two hours before class started, during which I planned out my instruction. After the school day, my work continued well into the evening hours, grading papers and assessing student learning ... only to do it all over again the next day. Perhaps you can relate.

That all changed when I began building my virtual course and discovering hacky ways to make technology work for me and my students. With each lesson I've built, I've learned more about technology and developed digital literacy skills that have directly helped me get my life back. As a result, I have completely redefined my practice by harnessing the power of technology to take back my mornings and nights, and I show other teachers how to do the same.

THE HACK: Fall in love with digital literacy

For many teachers, their love affair with edtech began when they realized they could go paperless and never ... ever ... have to stand in line at the copier again. It is reinforced when they realized they could, quite literally, save their hand from spending hours excruciatingly writing out comments on student papers and instead copy and paste comments into students' digitally uploaded work. While most of us started on our edtech journeys cautiously, we fall deeply in love with technology. As for me, I love the way my digital literacy makes everything teaching-related easier. If I wanted to, I could sing spelling words in a video and make the same video available to every class, every year. I could also write on a digital whiteboard to my heart's content and not get chalk dust up my nose.

With each new skill we develop, we become more efficient at our jobs. Our planning and grading become easier and less time-consuming, giving us the opportunity to fulfill our biological needs like using the bathroom (gasp!), eating lunch, or even taking a short walk for a brain breather. The internet is loaded with tools and workarounds for the menial tasks associated with teaching. To harness the power of technology, begin identifying the areas of your teaching that are difficult or time-consuming. Then take advantage of your device, apps, extensions, and keyboard shortcuts that can handle the tasks so you can focus on what you love about teaching: helping your students learn.

WHAT YOU CAN DO TOMORROW

- **Make a wish list**. Identify problems in your teaching life that you wish technology could fix for you. List them all out and group them by type. By listing what you would like to fix, you will be more focused and less overwhelmed when you explore technology options. It's likely that with each item on your wish list, you'll discover what Apple told us more than ten years ago:

"There's an app for that." (Yes, there's an app for someone to deliver a hot latte to you. Perhaps one day, it will be a built-in icon in your LMS.)

- **Search for apps and extensions in your LMS or streaming tool**. Open your Apple App store or Google Play app store, search for the name of your LMS or streaming tool, and look for extensions or apps that support it. Choose to investigate a few that may improve your teaching. You will be surprised by how many you will find. If you can't think of any search terms to help you find a solution to your problem, simply search education tech, and you will have access to extensions and apps that solve problems. Try out any that seem like they may fit your needs.

- **Ask your Professional Learning Network for help**. Post on Facebook or Twitter that you are looking for the best digital literacy skills to help make the tasks associated with teaching easier. Even if one person responds with one skill for you to consider, it's worth it. Perhaps that one skill will be a game-changer for you.

- **Subscribe to an educational podcast**. Numerous education podcasts are out there, ready for you to consume while driving, walking the dog, eating lunch, or making dinner. You can easily find podcasts with tech-savvy teachers discussing how they are using technology in their classrooms. Listen to find inspiration and with the intent of walking away with one new tip. Check out the Hack Learning Podcast at 10publications.com/podcast.

A BLUEPRINT FOR FULL IMPLEMENTATION

STEP 1: Know your device.

No matter what kind of device you are using to navigate your teaching, explore it and learn how to use it more fully to support the tasks associated with teaching. Begin by opening the settings of your device and exploring the categories to know what settings are available. For example, the **Accessibility Features** can make your device work more efficiently for you, such as a screen magnifier that helps with text visibility.

STEP 2: Learn new apps.

Explore free and inexpensive apps that will help you with your planning, teaching, and assessing. For example, mastering **Google's Workspace for Education** apps is well worth the time investment. After the learning curve, the right apps can make every facet of teaching easier.

STEP 3: Start adding extensions.

Extensions are designed to add functions and features to your browser to make your instruction, assessment, and organization more efficient. Whether you are looking to make your **Google Meet** more efficient or find a cool screencasting tool, extensions are a smart addition to your browser bar. To find helpful extensions, visit the Chrome web store (or your browser's web store) and look through the selections, which are categorized for easy reference. Check back often, as new extensions are created and added daily.

STEP 4: Learn keyboard shortcuts.

Even if you already use a handful of favorite keyboard shortcuts, such as Control-C to copy, this is a good time to see what other shortcuts are available. We all get comfortable with what we know and forget to look for something new, but keyboard short-cuts can save you a lot of time. Search online for your specific computer or device and a list of keyboard shortcuts. You can find diagrams and videos to help you learn which combinations work best for your device.

STEP 5: Make sure you know these basic and valuable digital skills.

You may already be a pro at these digital skills, or at least familiar with them, but scan the list to see if you can benefit by beefing up your skills in one of these areas.

- **Bookmarking:** Bookmarking allows you to save the address of a site for easier and quicker access to it. Once you save it, you can access it through your bookmark bar, located below the URL address, by clicking on an icon. This becomes par-ticularly useful when you visit the same site mul-tiple times a day. As teachers, we access our LMS courses and specific edtech throughout the day. Instead of searching for the site and signing in with a password each time, you can go right to it.

To bookmark, simply go to the address bar where the URL is located and click the star to the right of the bar. In addition, you can create folders on your bookmark bar and sync your bookmarks to all of your devices. Use bookmarking to organize your digital materials. For example, create a folder for each class you teach and bookmark all of the resources you access repeatedly.

- **Screenshots and snipping:** Taking a screenshot consists of using a key combo on your keyboard that takes a picture of your entire screen and creates a copy that you can save or paste somewhere else. A snipping tool is similar to a screenshot, but instead of taking a picture of the entire screen, it only captures the portion of the screen that you request. Screenshotting is a great way to save text and images that you want to access easily or manipulate for another purpose. To learn how to do this, search for the name of your device along with the words "screenshot" or "snipping." Different devices have different ways to do this.

- **Split screen:** A split screen allows you to split your screen into two different screens. This makes it easier to access two resources at the same time instead of having to switch between two tabs. I find it incredibly useful to transfer grades from one site into my online grade book. Instead of hopping between tabs, pulling it up on another device, or printing it out, I can simply split the screen and view the grades and my grade book simultaneously. To learn how to do this, search online for the name of your device or browser and the words "split screen."

Learning how to use tools that decrease the amount of time you spend on menial tasks will give you more time to focus on valuable tasks that make a difference in student learning.

- **Speech-to-text and text-to-speech:** All devices have accessibility features with speech-to-text and text-to-speech capabilities. You can also find apps and extensions that serve this purpose. Speech-to-text turns the words you say into words you can see. Essentially, it allows your voice to do the typing instead of your fingers. It's a great tool to access when you are grading and leaving comments for students. Text-to-speech turns words on the screen into words you can hear. This allows the computer to do the heavy lifting of reading and helps when it comes to reading research papers. A pro tip is to find one that lets you increase the playback speed. Then you can train yourself to understand and process the faster rate of speech. Doing so will allow you to cut your reading time in half, as your ears will process the material faster than your eyes ever could.

- **Hyperlinking:** This valuable skill allows you to attach a link to a word or image so the site associated with the link can be accessed with one click. Hyperlinking simply consists of highlighting a word or image and then right-clicking the highlighted area and selecting "hyperlink" or "insert link" into the word or image. Make it easy for everyone to access the materials you share.

OVERCOMING PUSHBACK

I was in third grade when my father proudly walked into our kitchen and placed a large, shiny black box on the counter. "It's a microwave," he boasted. Looking at my confused mother, he explained, "You can cook an entire family meal in just minutes." Annoyed by this new purchase, my mother walked away, shaking her head. For a full year, that microwave served as the biggest, shiniest clock in our house because the only function my technology-cautious mother would allow it to do was tell the time.

Then one day, it happened. It was dinnertime, and we were about to sit down to a delicious meal that included freshly baked bread. However, there was just one problem. My mother forgot to take out the butter to soften it in time for our meal. Faced with the reality that she would have to eat her fresh-baked bread dry and without butter, she turned to the microwave. At that moment, she realized the shiny black box was much more than an annoying impulse purchase. It had real potential to make her life easier. It didn't take much time for her to learn how to use the magic of the microwave to speed up her meal prep. It's been a staple in her house ever since. I share this story because you may not be using your device to its full potential, but if you try out one of the hacks in this book, you may find that it's magical and will make your life easier, just like a microwave. The following pushbacks remind me of my pre-microwave mother. They represent educators who may need encouragement to soften the butter and give a new tech tool a try.

I don't want to become too dependent on technology. If you are fearful that technology is consuming every aspect of your life and you don't want to rely on it any more than you have to, I would say education is *not* the tech-free hill you want to die on. Sure, skip the smart light bulbs at home if you want, but embrace technology as an educator to benefit you and your students. The reality is that our time is limited. Learning how to use tools that decrease the amount of time you spend on menial tasks, like entering grades or organizing resources, will give you more time to focus on valuable tasks that make a difference in student learning. As teachers, we always have ideas we would love to implement because we know it would help student learning, but we often don't have the time. If you can shift your thinking from relying on technology to do your job to using technology to make you a better teacher, you will likely feel more positive about what technology can do for you.

I'm just not a tech person. In the beginning, there were no tech people. Being tech-savvy is not a natural character trait. It's a learned skill that develops slowly over time. When you learn each new trick of the trade, your tech skills and intuition strengthen. Don't be afraid to admit you don't know something or to ask for help. The first time I went online, I asked a seventh grader for help. I was serving as a teaching assistant in a computer class, and I got tired of acting like I knew what I was doing. So, I turned to one of my students. I've been online ever since. If your reluctance to embrace technology in your teaching comes from a place of self-doubt, then I am here to tell you that you can do it. You can be a tech person and find the support you need as you grow your skills.

THE HACK IN ACTION

Kerin Steigerwalt is a middle school English teacher who has presented about digital literacy skills at the state and national levels. She shares the tricks of her trade with her wildly popular Girls Gone Google presentation.

She reflects on her transition to virtual learning in 2020 and is grateful she already had strong digital literacy skills. Steigerwalt used **Form Mule** to send out bulk personalized emails each week, and she used extensions like **Permanent Clipboard** that allowed her to create robust comments that she could access with a right-click. These two tools changed her grading life by saving her time each day.

Steigerwalt recognizes that it can be overwhelming for teachers to develop their digital literacy skills. She advises that they take it slow by integrating tools that can help solve problems. "There are so many amazing digital tools out there, and it's easy to be distracted by the latest 'oooh, shiny' one. Knowing what outcomes you want will allow you to focus less on sorting through a smorgasbord of tools and more on applying the right one for the occasion."

Like many teachers, when Steigerwalt shifted to an online format, she was concerned about giving assignments that students could easily cheat on. She learned that technology, such as **Google educational apps**, could help her create her own learning artifacts that assess at a higher depth of knowledge to solve the problem of cheating.

"As a language arts teacher, one of the challenges is getting kids to show they understand a novel without just giving them reading comprehension questions to complete that are 'Googleable.'" Instead, she uses **Google Slides** to create an activity in which students categorize the elements of the story in a way that makes sense to them and demonstrates learning without cheating. See Images 10.1 and 10.2.

Directions

1. On the next slide, you will see four pink boxes, a blue box, and lots of yellow boxes around the outside.

2. Your job is to sort the yellow boxes into four different categories.

3. The pink boxes all have a white spot for you to label your categories. These should be words YOU type, NOT yellow boxes.

4. Once you have sorted out the yellow boxes into the categories you chose, explain WHY you sorted them that way in the blue box. YES, you must make FOUR categories – no more, no less; YES, you must use ALL the yellow boxes.

5. When you are done with ALL of that, you may delete this slide and submit your work.

6. If you do not finish in class, this is homework, and it is due by the end of today.

Image 10.1: Steigerwalt created these instructions for her assessment to determine her students' reading comprehension skills.

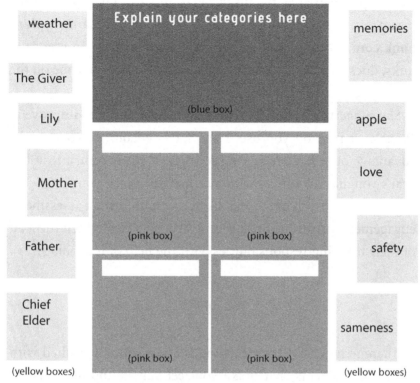

weather

Explain your categories here

memories

The Giver

Lily

(blue box)

apple

love

Mother

(pink box)　(pink box)

Father

safety

Chief
Elder

sameness

(yellow boxes)　(pink box)　(pink box)　(yellow boxes)

Image 10.2: Google Slides provided the assessment platform for students to demonstrate their learning without the possibility of cheating.

Steigerwalt also describes how technology can help keep her middle school students engaged in an online class. She says they struggle with having an online presence during synchronous meetings. So, she generates enthusiasm with the press of a button.

"This might sound goofy, but I use the **Confetti Cannon Add-On in Chrome** to do simple little confetti tosses any time a kid gives an outstanding answer, or we have perfect attendance, or really any time I feel like it. It's something little and fun, and I don't use it every day or every minute, but when I do, we all get a smile."

Finally, Steigerwalt uses technology to solve the ultimate

teacher problem area: planning. "Planning can take a lot of time if you're not purposeful about it. I use a digital planner, **planbook.com**, so that I can gather all of my resources in one spot: links, docs, articles, videos, etc. It saves me a TON of time on the day of the lesson."

She suggests all teachers reflect on their practice to improve it. "Whatever method you use, I absolutely encourage you to take advantage of reflection in a space you can easily return to—'last year's you' has a lot of good advice for 'this year's you'!"

Whether it is solving problems of communication, assessment, engagement, planning, or reflecting, teachers can lighten the load of their teaching responsibilities with the help of technology.

There is no doubt that teaching is a rewarding job filled with beautiful moments that make you feel valued and appreciated. However, those moments can quickly be forgotten by the burden of the numerous tasks associated with teaching. Developing digital literacy skills is time-consuming and requires exploration, but it will pay off as you learn how to make planning, teaching, assessing, and grading easier. Sure, you use edtech already, but by cracking your heart open and embracing the awesome power of technology, you can fall in love with teaching again, both in person and on a screen.

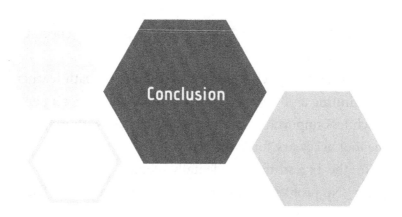

Conclusion

TIME TO BUILD

I can only show you the door. You're the one who has to walk through it.

—MORPHEUS IN *THE MATRIX*, BY LANA AND LILLY WACHOWSKI

W E HAVE THE greatest job in the world, and one thing that makes it so great is that we had a twelve-year internship before we took our first college-level education course. As students, we had a decade-long front-row seat at good and bad teaching. In real time, through constant exposure, we learned what works and what does not. As a result, we acquired an innate understanding of best practices before we ever stepped foot into a leadership role as classroom teachers. No other profession has a more prepared workforce.

Throughout the day, so many little problems need to be solved, and we naturally solve them with very little thought because we've seen it done a hundred times.

From the little stuff: "No pencil? No problem, check the cup by the sharpener."

I learned that trick from my seventh grade math teacher, who felt winning a power struggle over a kid who forgot a pencil was much less important than providing the kid with easy access to the tool necessary for learning.

To the big stuff: "Accidentally stapled your finger to your paper? No problem, grab the trash can and your best friend and head to the nurse."

I learned that trick from my third grade teacher when my best friend stapled her finger to a paper. She understood that even an accident with blood involved can seem like fun if you have your best friend with you. As for the trash can, let's just say the teacher understood the impact of seeing your best friend with a paper stapled to her finger.

The point is, we can innately respond to these little and big problems that pop up because we've seen our teachers respond to the same situations. For the most part, we don't even have to think about them because those experiences are embedded in our brain, and our practiced responses are natural. When we reach a problem, we simply call on this embedded experience and get the kids back on track. We can support them, make them feel good about themselves, and motivate them with these learned intangibles that are so critical in teaching.

That gets taken away when we go online.

Not one of us has twelve years of experience as a virtual student that we can draw on innately without thinking about how to handle a specific situation, whether it's motivation, engagement, or checking for understanding. Going virtual has made what we do no longer natural. That means to be successful, we must now be intentional about our practice. We can no longer rely on this wealth of experience to help resolve problems as they pop up.

When I started my virtual journey in 2013, I did so alone. Because of the innovative nature of the course, there were few resources to help guide my practice. I had no mentor, no instructional coach, no lesson samples, and no research on best practices. I just had my passion for teaching and a relentless desire to succeed. There was nobody to teach me the technology associated with delivering an online course, and there was definitely nobody able to teach me about online pedagogy. My administration supported my program, but they didn't really understand the experience I was trying to create. To be honest, neither did I. My class was nicknamed Hollie and the Holograms.

Several years later, watching my colleagues navigate the new world of pandemic teaching, I was reminded again of the *Supermarket Sweep* panic of my early teaching days, and I am here to tell you: *It gets better.* By it, I mean all of it. Your use of technology and your ability to understand your objective, deliver content, and assess student learning will evolve and improve. The panic will fade, and you will be armed with a new skill set that will redefine your teaching.

Dr. Ruben Puentedura's SAMR (substitution, augmentation, modification, and redefinition) model categorizes four degrees of classroom technology integration. The model is intended to assess the role that technology plays in lesson design. However, it speaks to the journey that I endeavored to take when I created my virtual classroom in which I systematically evolved through the four distinct stages.

Early in the creation of my virtual classroom, I was trying to substitute what I was doing in my face-to-face classroom.

Essentially, my goal was to use the technology to create the same learning experiences my face-to-face students were receiving. So if my face-to-face students received a thirty-minute lecture, my virtual students received a recording of the thirty-minute lecture. If my face-to-face students received a worksheet, then my virtual students received a digital copy of the worksheet.

When the pandemic forced teachers into a virtual learning model, I saw many of my colleagues do the same substitution, which was totally appropriate given their inexperience with virtual learning. However, I also learned in my early teaching that this did not yield the highest learning outcomes because, while I can recreate the same content and learning artifacts in a digital setting, I can't substitute the nuanced unmeasurable parts of face-to-face teaching. Those nuances cannot be duplicated in a virtual setting by simply digitizing the materials associated with the learning tasks.

Fortunately, with time, my technological skills improved. Teaching virtual classes forced me to experiment with various online learning tools, and as my understanding of these tools increased, I developed numerous virtual instructional strategies. As a result, my face-to-face and virtual teaching practices have evolved through the SAMR model. Currently, my practice firmly straddles modification and redefinition because I am using technology to significantly modify the look and feel of my face-to-face courses into a fully functioning blended classroom. I have also redefined my classroom into a fully functioning virtual class.

Most importantly, my evolution has completely changed the look and feel of my virtual course. My practice is deliberate and methodically planned with an awareness of my learning objectives, online instructional strategies, digital tools, and student learning goals. My objective with this book is to help accelerate that process for you.

When schools closed and we dove into virtual learning, my assistant superintendent said she was frustrated by the lack of research on evidence-based virtual teaching practices. She knew about my virtual teaching success and reached out to me to discuss what resources I used to build my virtual course and online teaching skills. I said I didn't use any because there weren't any. She wasn't the only one who sent me a distress signal. Multiple organizations asked me to share my experience and provide a vision to help guide teachers through this uncharted world of pandemic teaching.

Hacking Flex Teaching will help you during this transition and beyond by using my years of virtual teaching experience to anticipate the problems you are experiencing and provide easy-to-implement solutions that prevent the problem from ever occurring.

Mastering your LMS will help solve the problem of creating a classroom without a classroom. Investing time in learning how to use it will help you create a virtual space where teachers and students can manage their learning.

Using templates, routines, and protocols to establish consistent communication will create an environment in which all stakeholders feel safe, heard, and validated. Nothing is more important than student voice, and it is critical that you create communication norms so all students feel that their voice is valued.

Getting to know your students is difficult in virtual learning. However, being intentional about getting to know them by embedding engagement into your lesson design and schedule will help dissolve the screen and create the authentic relationships necessary to cultivate learning.

Plotting your pedagogy by adopting the Gradual Release of Responsibility was a complete game-changer for my virtual instruction. It gave me a reliable pedagogical map that I could follow when I built my course. It will be an invaluable decision that will not only support your decision-making as you plan but result in student mastery.

Choosing to strategize your instructional strategies by selecting tools that meet your and your students' needs is a critical first step in learning to harness the power of educational technology. Learning should never be about the flash and appeal of a tool, but rather anchored in strong, pedagogically sound decision-making that supports your style and student needs.

Assessing your assessment to reimagine how to use student data to make instructional decisions is strong pedagogical practice and a key component to twenty-first-century best practices. We must work to reframe negative feelings about assessment because, with strong instructional strategies and the Gradual Release of Responsibility to plot student learning, assessments will become a critical tool in your educational arsenal.

Once you have learned to master your LMS and plot your pedagogy, creating personalized learning pathways is the next powerful step in transforming education. Being able to unite technology and strong pedagogy to give every student exactly what they need, at the exact moment they need it, and for as long as they need it helps generate much-needed educational equity.

Another awesome byproduct of our innovation is the ability to apply technology to create the least restrictive environment to support special education students. Students can begin to feel like empowered learners by being taught how to use technology to support their needs.

Preparing for flex teaching will require much work and planning. However, by economizing your efficiency, you can make sound pedagogical decisions that strike a balance between building, planning, and instruction, and allow you to have a personal life (yes!).

Finally, embracing the awesome power of technology by learning how to use your device, extensions, and apps to make your job easier will be the spoonful of sugar that will make all this work and transition go down in a worthwhile way.

The reality is that all teachers were grossly underprepared for this emergency endeavor. Without the resources, training, and vision to guide us, all we could do was try to get by, just like my mom did when the layoffs started and she had to serve our family *you know what* on a shingle. We did the best we could with what we had and served up lessons that closely resembled that SOS. However, as we move forward into what will undoubtedly be a flexible teaching environment, our kids deserve better than our "try to get by."

Fortunately, my prediction that someday I would be replaced by a robot teacher, which was the impetus for me developing my edtech skills, has not happened ... yet. However, while we are not in a direct existential crisis, as educators, we must recognize the significance of this moment. Critical decisions with long-term implications are being made at the speed of light. We cannot allow this time to pass us by without having a voice in that decision-making process. We must be willing to innovate our practice, embrace twenty-first-century best practices, and prove that teachers, not technology, are capable of solving the problems of teaching and learning. We do that by proving we are "flex teachers" surviving pandemic teaching by thriving at flex teaching.

ABOUT THE AUTHOR

PASSIONATE ABOUT EDUCATIONAL innovation and equity, Hollie Woodard, 2022 Pennsylvania Teacher of the Year Finalist, is a special needs parent, English teacher, and tech coach from Pennsylvania's Council Rock School District. She serves as the Advocacy Chair of The Pennsylvania Association for Educational Communications and Technology (PAECT) and advocates for digital equity.

As the founder of the Pennsylvania Dyslexia Teacher Taskforce, she advocates for literacy by educating teachers about the inequity of dyslexia. She also serves on the Pennsylvania Teacher Advisory Committee (PTAC), where she shares her narratives to help drive educational decision-making in the state. As a Keystone Technology Innovator Star and Lead Learner, she works to innovate public education by advocating for twenty-first-century best practices.

She and her husband, Ryan, have been happily married for twenty years and are the proud and exhausted parents of two boys. Their happy little family can be found every Saturday night at their local Chili's, where it is their family tradition to receive outstanding service from their favorite waitress, Tina, while sipping strawberry margaritas and losing horribly at trivia. You can connect with her on Twitter @holliewood24.

ACKNOWLEDGMENTS

TIMES 10 PUBLICATIONS: Thank you for seeing value in my work and giving me the amazing opportunity to contribute to education. Jennifer Jas, thank you for your confidence in me and my work and for helping me see the forest from the trees. Jennifer Zelinger Marshall, thank you so much for getting my jokes ... and catching all of my writing mistakes was pretty cool too! Steven Plummer, thank you for creating a cover that captured the spirit of the book and symbolized everything that was important to me.

Mom: Thank you for saving your pennies to buy me that teacher doll for Christmas. You never once doubted I came here to teach. You always believe in me, even when I can't.

Dad: Thank you for teaching me to be fearless. It's easy to have courage with you standing behind me.

Ryan: Everything I have, we created together. Even though there ain't no sunshine when I'm gone, you selflessly share me with the world. All of my lovely days have been with you. Thank you for this life, the boys, folding the laundry, and my Zoomie.

Jake: I had no voice until you gave me a story to tell. Thank you for always courageously giving me permission to tell it. Always remember, we are not defined by the stories our parents tell. You are so much more than any narrative I could tell. I love you more.

Dean: You are the true writer and artist in the family. I can't wait to see how you share your talents with the world. Thanks for your patience with me ... I promise I'm almost done. I'll watch you play Fortnite, and you can finally teach me Minecraft. You are my sunshine.

Group Chat: You are my ride or die. I don't survive this without you.

Berger & Jon: Big and Little Spoon, you always see me better than I am. Your belief in me has given me the confidence to believe I can do this, but seriously, I'm not a Boomer.

KTI: Life-changing, to say the least. My little advocacy adventure continues to grow because you encouraged me to find my voice. Scott, the depth of your impact on me and education in Pennsylvania is immeasurable. Mama, doing my best to share my shine.

Decoding Dyslexia PA: Keep doing the work because the kids and their parents need you.

Mrs. Arndt: You were right; I can write. You were taken too soon, but so many of us teach because of you. The world is a little kinder because of you.

Special thanks to the outstanding educators who contributed their narrative to this book.

Ryan, you will forever be my favorite six-foot-three-inch male kindergarten teacher. Thank you for generously sharing your thoughtful practices with me and the world. Thank you for sharing your friendship with me ... you are my favorite purple person!

Liz: The Donald to my Mickey and the U to my Q, my car ride

home phone call, you complete me, my friend! Thank you for saying yes to every adventure. I'm so proud of the way you have worked to innovate physical education! Thank you for sharing your work in this book.

John: I am in constant amazement of your generosity and willingness to share yourself with the world. Our relationship consists of me asking you for something and you ALWAYS saying yes. I'm thrilled to have your voice in my book, and I am so very appreciative of the work you do to change the game for all kids.

Jess: You are my unicorn spirit animal! Thank you so much for sharing your awesome work with me in this book. Your innate compassion for everyone you meet makes you an outstanding educator, as your desire to get things right comes from love.

Christina: My favorite Diva! I am so excited to have your energy in this book. I love talking shop with you, and I am so thankful that teachers will have even more access to the thoughtful work you are doing.

Joe: Thank you for serving as a mentor to me through the PATOY process. You have done amazing work to support education in Pennsylvania, and I am excited that you have generously shared your practice with me for this book so teachers around the world can learn from you.

Colleen: Thank you for lending your expertise and voice to this book. You are doing innovative and exciting work that will result in learning equity.

Kelly: Thank you for making me a better teacher. Our discussions on education push my thinking and recharge my batteries. I am constantly inspired by your endless passion and relentless desire to get it right for our most vulnerable students. All of the solutions to education's problems can be found echoing off the walls of 232 East.

Kerin: Nobody Googles better than you! Thanks for sharing your expertise. No doubt, your ideas will help provide some much-needed relief for teachers!

A million thanks to the outstanding students who helped me find my way. Whether virtual or face-to-face, I always get the best students. Your willingness to learn with me is the reason I've been able to innovate my teaching and why I was able to write this book. Special thanks to Barry Desko, Andrea Houston-Lingman, Susan McCarthy, and Jason Traczykiewicz, who saw the value in empowering student learning with choice and gave me the unprecedented opportunity to turn my vision into reality. Finally, special thanks to my Virtual Sister, Althea Tomlinson, who has shared in every virtual triumph and heartbreak and is equally responsible for the success of our virtual program.

MORE FROM TIMES 10

Browse all titles at 10Publications.com

Hacking School Discipline
9 Ways to Create a Culture of Empathy & Responsibility Using Restorative Justice
By Nathan Maynard and Brad Weinstein

Reviewers proclaim this *Washington Post* Bestseller to be "maybe the most important book a teacher can read, a must for all educators, fabulous, a game changer!" Teachers and presenters Nathan Maynard and Brad Weinstein demonstrate how to eliminate punishment and build a culture of responsible students and independent learners in a book that will become your new blueprint for school discipline. Eighteen straight months at #1 on Amazon and still going strong, *Hacking School Discipline* is disrupting education like nothing we've seen in decades—maybe centuries.

Hacking Engagement
50 Tips & Tools to Engage Teachers and Learners Daily
By James Alan Sturtevant

If you're a teacher who appreciates quick ideas to engage your students, this is the book for you. *Hacking Engagement* provides fifty unique, exciting, and actionable tips and tools that you can apply right now. Try one of these amazing engagement strategies tomorrow: engage the enraged, create celebrity couple nicknames, hash out a hashtag, avoid the war on yoga pants, let your freak flag fly, become a proponent of the exponent, and transform your class into a focus group. Are you ready to engage?

Browse all titles at 10Publications.com

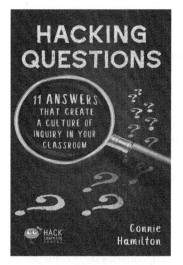

Hacking Questions
11 Answers that Create a Culture of
Inquiry in Your Classroom
By Connie Hamilton

Questions are the driving force of learning in classrooms, but teachers have questions about how to engage their students with the art of questioning. *Hacking Questions* digs into framing, delivering, and maximizing questions in the classroom to keep students engaged in learning. Known in education circles as the "Questioning Guru," Connie Hamilton shows teachers of all subjects and grades how to ask the questions that deliver not just answers but reflection, metacognition, and real learning.

Project Based Learning
Real Questions. Real Answers. How to
Unpack PBL and Inquiry
By Ross Cooper and Erin Murphy

Educators would love to leverage project based learning to create learner-centered opportunities for their students, but why isn't PBL the norm? Because teachers have questions. *Project Based Learning* is Ross Cooper and Erin Murphy's response to the most common and complex questions educators ask about PBL and inquiry, including: How do I structure a PBL experience? How do I get grades? How do I include direct instruction? What happens when kids don't work well together? Learn how to teach with PBL and inquiry in any subject or grade.

Browse all titles at 10Publications.com

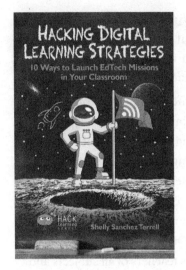

Hacking Digital Learning Strategies
10 Ways to Launch EdTech Missions in Your Classroom
By Shelly Sanchez Terrell

Teachers need strategies to bring the power of digital learning to their classrooms. In this book, international EdTech presenter and NAPW Woman of the Year Shelly Sanchez Terrell demonstrates EdTech Missions—lessons and projects that inspire learners to use web tools and social media to innovate, research, collaborate, problem-solve, campaign, crowdfund, crowdsource, and publish. She includes a thirty-eight-page Mission Toolkit complete with reproducible mission cards, badges, polls, and other handouts that you can copy and distribute to students immediately.

Hacking Instructional Design
33 Extraordinary Ways to Create a Contemporary Curriculum
By Michael Fisher and Elizabeth Fisher

Whether you want to make subtle changes to your instructional design or turn it on its head—*Hacking Instructional Design* provides a toolbox of options. Discover just-in-time tools to design, upgrade, or adapt your teaching strategies, lesson plans, and unit plans. These strategies offer you the power and permission to be the designer, not the recipient, of a contemporary curriculum. Students and teachers will benefit for years to come when you apply these engaging tools starting tomorrow.

Browse all titles at 10Publications.com

RESOURCES FROM TIMES 10

Nurture your inner educator:
10publications.com/educatortype

Podcasts:
hacklearningpodcast.com
jamesalansturtevant.com/podcast

On Twitter:
@10Publications
@HackMyLearning
#Times10News
#WhatsBestForKids
#RealPBL
@LeadForward2
#LeadForward
#HackLearning
#HackingLeadership
#MakeWriting
#HackingQs
#HackingSchoolDiscipline
#LeadWithGrace
#QuietKidsCount
#ModernMentor
#AnxiousBook
#HackYourLibrary

All things Times 10:
10publications.com

TIMES 10 provides practical solutions that busy educators can read today and use tomorrow. We bring you content from experienced teachers and leaders, and we share it through books, podcasts, webinars, articles, events, and ongoing conversations on social media. Our books and materials help turn practice into action. Stay in touch with us at 10Publications.com and follow our updates on Twitter @10Publications and #Times10News.

Made in the USA
Monee, IL
15 October 2023

44639534R00116